The Great Landmark Race

Tourism for designers and landmark design for tourists.

By Christopher J. Elliott

Published in Australia by:

Place Research Institute
Address: PO Box 12266, Abeckett Street VIC 8006, Australia
Email: PlaceResearchInstitute@outlook.com

First published in Australia 2020
Copyright © Christopher J Elliott 2020

All rights reserved. No part of this publication may be reproduced, stored in a retrieval system, or transmitted, in any form or by any means without the prior written permission of the publisher, nor be otherwise circulated in any form of binding or cover other than that in which it is published and without a similar condition being imposed on the subsequent purchaser.

National Library of Australia Cataloguing.

A catalogue record for this book is available from the National Library of Australia

Paperback ISBN: 978-0-6489556-2-7
Epub ISBN: 978-0-6489556-3-4

Cover layout and design by Akit Fong

Disclaimer
All care has been taken in the preparation of the information herein, but no responsibility can be accepted by the publisher or author for any damages resulting from the misinterpretation of this work. All contact details given in this book were current at the time of publication, but are subject to change.

The advice given in this book is based on the experience of the individuals. Professionals should be consulted for individual problems. The author and publisher shall not be responsible for any person with regard to any loss or damage caused directly or indirectly by the information in this book.

Contents

Preface 4
1. Isolation 7
2. The Great Bucket List 20
3. Landmarks 37
4. The Race 50
5. The Race for Tall 63
6. Big Things 96
7. The Race for Meaning 118
8. The Race to be Memorable 148
9. The Opinion List 172
10. The Score 187
11. The Results 195
12. Winning the Race 222
The Ranking 239
Bibliography 259
About the Author 272
Author Contact 272
Acknowledgments 273

Preface

This book is written in 2020 as the world goes through the COVID19 crisis. My country, Australia, is recovering from catastrophic bush fires, there are racial equality demonstrations in the streets, and dictators are cementing their power. Two years ago, the tourism industry saw one-fifth of the world's population travel for leisure. Now, many people are not allowed to leave their homes. The industry has gone from 9.25 trillion dollars down to virtually nothing within a couple of months.

The positive side of this crisis is to now take the time for reflection. We have been so busy doing things, we have not had time to think about *why*.

For the first time in my thirty years of working as an urban designer specialising in tourism, I have stopped to take a breath. I have worked in over 25 countries, flying in and out in a day, or settling down for months. I have had meetings in Cairo, where I skipped out early to see the Great Pyramids. I have spent weeks exploring 52 islands in Koh Chang evaluating resorts for the Sustainable Tourism Department of Thailand. I have had the good fortune of designing a region for the PyeongChang Winter Olympics (originally for 2014 but was won for 2018). I have flown so much around the world the tubes in my ears have collapsed from the pressure changes, causing them to pop every few seconds – all day, every day.

Throughout my travels I had planned on pulling this book together. The stories you will read, I noted down at the time hoping they would be in this book. During my Master's degree in Tourism, I asked questions in seminars, as notes for these chapters. I have collected raw data on thousands of landmarks for over ten years and input it into an Excel spreadsheet on my phone, to one day have time to analyse it and see what it reveals.

The Landmark Race is a story about this exploration. I hope you find exciting all the amazing places in the world as much as I do. I also hope you find interesting the great architectural landmarks, natural landmarks, the sculptures, roadside attractions and oddities our planet has available to visit. You do not need to be a designer who creates landmarks to understand them, you can be a tourist, as I am too, and visit these places.

The Great Landmark Race answers a question that only reflection can reveal, and that is the question of *why*. Why civilisations build monuments to people, our gods, and our corporations. It is about a race to be the tallest, to be the biggest, to have meaning and to be memorable. It is a race for attention, acknowledgement, fame. It is a never-ending race with each location striving to compete with everywhere else. Yet this race is optimistic. It is not about destruction, war, or disease. It is about inspiration and creation. It is about the greatest places on Earth and how every corner has something unique and inspirational in it.

Christopher J. Elliott

Melbourne, July 2020

1. Isolation

"Alone we can do so little; together we can do so much." Helen Keller

Landmarks attract people and can be a cure for isolation. Ten thousand years ago, humanity began as small groups of isolated tribes living in caves. Today, we have worked together to build civilisations that reach the sky and house millions of people. Societies have grown, collapsed, and flourished, leaving behind the apex of their existence as a landmark.

A landmark survives through a human selection process. Civilisations destroy architecture they dislike or do not use, and they protect architecture they consider to be great; this is known as heritage protection today. Throughout time, people have come out of their isolation, banded together and built landmarks – all around the globe. Modern Rome has at its centre, the Colosseum, standing for two thousand years. London has the one-thousand-year-old Tower of London, and Kyoto has the 600-year-old Temple of the Golden Pavilion, Kinkaku-ji.

The great landmark race is all about us; the human race, and its fight to survive, to grow and to prosper. It is about all the world's cultures moving forward throughout history, to expand global knowledge, to go further, higher, bigger, with more ingenuity and more creativity than those before them. Landmarks predate books and movies. They tell stories of the past when languages are lost or forgotten. To experience a landmark, you cannot curl up in bed and simply read, or sit in a dark movie theatre and watch. You must buy a ticket, organise a place to stay, then go. You can then climb the landmark's steps, you can touch its stone walls, or you may sit in a café and view it on the horizon. If a landmark was a book, then tourism is the act of reading that book.

Landmarks act as a beacon to tourists, pulling people from all over the world to see them. They stand as a monument to the achievements of its civilisation. It happens today, with the world's tallest building, the Burj Khalifa in Dubai, or in previous dynasties with the Forbidden City in Beijing.

Yet this book is written in 2020 during the COVID19 pandemic when tourism has collapsed. We are back in a type of tribal isolation. Some see other countries as enemies rather than tourist destinations. With international borders closed, suspicion and paranoia have replaced cultural exchange and economic cooperation.

For the first time in history, the function of a landmark – to lure visitors, wealth, prestige, power and fame to a city – is obsolete. The tourism industry has gone from 9.25 trillion US dollars globally down to near zero with less wealthy people and countries suffering the most. In many places, it is illegal to travel, compared to 2018 when 1.4 billion people travelled, as tourists, to elsewhere in the world[1]. That is one-fifth of the world's population. These people packed their bags, got on a train, bus or plane, travelled somewhere else, shopped, relaxed, visited a landmark and then went home. Our world is so connected that a Coronavirus can spread throughout the planet in a month. Before this crisis, an Australian found it cheaper to go to Bali for a week than to visit another state. For the British, airfares to Spain were less expensive than a train ticket to the next city, and for Hong Kongers, travel to Thailand was cheaper than a luxury city hotel.

This connectedness had the added advantage of bringing about global equality by dispersing wealth around the world. A landmark can pull tourists to more impoverished locations, bringing with them their tourist dollars. A supermarket in a town with a landmark can do far better with the addition of tourists than it can by relying only on the local population. Tourists add to the local economy, which means more staff, more jobs, and a more comprehensive range of products. It can stay open later, creating a benefit to everyone in the town. It is easier for places to bring in tourists than it is to mine resources or manufacture products.

Compared to other industries, tourism has the added advantage of being more environmentally sustainable. Tourism brings with it a win for locals, for visitors, the environment, and the economy.

Free Independent Travellers (FIT) are visitors that vacation on their own, preferring not to travel in tour groups. They will explore anywhere of interest and tend to disperse their wealth in lesser-known places in the world. All they need is a rental car, or in some cases only hiking boots, to travel. The more they visit a location, the more friends they tell, Instagram and Facebook posts they make, and the more famous the landmarks become.

A tourism location may begin as a small backpacker retreat near a landmark waterfall or temple in a hidden mountain village. The more tourists are attracted to this location, the more facilities for tourists that get developed. These facilities may include better hotels, shops, and other activities. Eventually, a place will grow into a series of attractions and in some cases, into resorts and theme parks with improved roads and transport. The final stage of development is a new airport creating a tourism hub. It is known as *scalability* in the tourism industry. Places can quickly scale up to meet the inflow of tourists and their needs. Yet, from a westerner's perspective, this could be thought of as a negative impact. The feeling that a remote village can transition into a mass tourism hub gives many people a sense of unease. It feels as though the local culture is washed away and a bland global culture is put in its place. It may be saddening to some. It is a form of cultural contamination, and in the era of COVID19, this mirrors viral contamination.

One of the last places in the world to still be isolated is North Sentinel Island in the Andaman Sea between India and Myanmar. The island is a protectorate of India. A visit in 1967 found around 80 to 150 people, with current estimates guessing the population to be anywhere between 15 to 500. The villagers all live a simple lifestyle in small lean-to huts all facing each other. This would provide little privacy. They have a communal fire pit where the tribe gathers at night. People carve out canoes for fishing between the protective reef and the shoreline. They craft bows, arrows, spears and knives for use in hunting turtles, wild pigs and birds. They also collect bird eggs, fruit, and underground tubers[2]. It is illegal, under India's laws, to get within 10 kilometres of the island.

In 1880 an expedition lead by Maurice Vidal Portman visited the island and captured an older man, his wife, and their four children. The man and woman had been protected by the island's isolation from the outsider's disease. Once they were exposed to other people, they eventually got sick and died. The four orphaned children were now more of a burden, so they were sent back to the island[3]. It is unknown if, or how many people died from any diseases the children brought with them as there was no further contact with the island until 2019.

In that year, a 26-year-old Christian missionary, John Chau, wanted to bring Christianity to the island, so he paid local fishermen to take him there. Minutes after landing, he was killed by arrows, and the fishermen reported seeing his body being dragged around by the inhabitants. The seven fishermen involved in transporting John were arrested for participation in the visit. Again, it is unknown how many people got sick or died from this visit. The tribespeople appear to know that outsiders bring death and the killing was more of an act of self-defence than of murder.

Alternatively, some people do not wish to be isolated.

To assist in developing China every few years, the government launches a *Five-Year Plan*. In 2009 the plan was to develop rural areas, and the design team and I were hired by the Provincial Government to develop a valley in the eastern part of Yunnan Province. China develops its rural areas in a different way to other countries. Instead of the process used in the west, of creating activities for tourists, then building hotels and accommodation, then improving roads, building train lines and finally an airport, as demand increases, the Chinese Government does the exact opposite.

The airport was constructed first and to facilitate it, the top of a mountain was bulldozed and pushed into the neighbouring valley, creating the only flat area of land. It had one flight a week at the time, and due to its location in the clouds, it was common for it to get cancelled due to storms. The airport's height caused lightning to strike along eye level. It was frightening seeing horizontal lightning bounce across the tarmac. I was happy to have my flight repeatedly cancelled. The freeway infrastructure was also built, bringing a divided road right up to the boundary of the valley. It reduced from a four-lane freeway to a dirt track with an incredible bump. Their development approach of infrastructure first and attractions last, is quite brilliant. For when travel time is reduced, demand skyrockets. Our role was to create a tourism landmark for this valley and to plan hotels, resorts, and attractions. We spent weeks travelling around the one hundred square kilometre valley to find places of interest and think of activities for people to participate.

There was a reservoir that had some of those giant wheeled, floating tricycles that paddle around. We were told it was the region's first tourism attraction. I smirked but did not comment. Far more interesting were some semi-flooded caves where you enter by boat and paddle amongst gigantic stalagmites and stalactites as you loop through the cave system and back out to a natural lake that looked like a garden of Eden. The valley was surrounded by stone-cast mountains that appeared like old Chinese watercolour paintings. The views were spectacular. There was a winery with wine that tasted like grape juice, so sweet you can feel your teeth rot. The streetlights were shaped like chillies in celebration of the chillies grown in the valley, and there were two disused quarries devastating the sides of mountains.

As a westerner in China, I felt uneasy at developing a landmark attraction and a tourism destination that would pull people in from around the world to this quiet, forgotten valley. I was aware of the cultural contamination that was soon to change these people's quiet farming life into a mass tourism hub. Are these people like the North Sentinel Island villages not wanting visitors? Was I being condescending? As an outsider, it was not my choice to make. So, I asked the provincial administrator about engaging with the local people.

In democratic countries, we go through a public consultation process where we conduct surveys, interviews or show designs to the community, to understand their opinions of a project. I found it challenging working in China, with the government pushing on with projects without hearing locals' thoughts. Do they even want the development? The fact is that China can do things very quickly without consultation, and this is how they have managed to move a billion people out of poverty – one of the most significant achievements in human history in the shortest amount of time. The question I had was if it could be done better using a different process.

To satisfy my doubts, the administrator took me to the closest farmhouse and asked, *"Will this house do?"*

He went up and spoke to the farmers who instantly invited us in for lunch. Their house was made of mud brick and had a well-worn dirt floor that was hard as stone. The only door to the house had a threshold to step over, similar to old temples, and was painted red with an ornate knocker. There were only two rooms with the main room used for dining with a lounge area and a bedroom at the back, and the other room was the kitchen. Our host pulled up extra seats to a large round table in the centre. A woman ran around putting things away in cupboards and boxes while turning off the television. Another woman called from the kitchen for bits and pieces she needed for the meal. The other end of the room had beds which looked like army cots, and there was an alcove sleeping area with a standard double bed.

I put my head around the corner into the kitchen to notice it was very dark with the only light coming from between the top of the mud-brick walls and the metal roof. The wok was the size of a truck wheel, and sat on a wood fire that was threatening to burn the whole province down. The cooking was causing so much smoke, it made sense the only other room would be a kitchen. We ate a very spicy lunch (it took my tongue a week to heal), and we even tried the local delicacy of fried bees. Very crunchy by the way, tasted like potato crisps without the food additives.

We eventually got to talking about their opinion of the project to develop a landmark tourist attraction in the valley. It turned out the local council had made some pretty bad investments and lost a lot of money, requiring the Provincial Government to step in and hire us to help develop the area. (As a side note, there is a village in China where the council put all their money on the stock exchange and won, making all the townspeople millionaires.) The results of this loss meant the valley had poor water quality, health services, and everyone lived as subsistence farmers, earning just enough money to survive.

It was not long before our host became very opinionated and angry, helped along with the potent rice wine.

"Why does everyone in China become rich, and we stay poor?" The man gestured towards the television. *"We have tried to grow tobacco and vegetables, many things, but nothing makes enough money."*

"Would you like to work in a hotel?" I asked the man.

"No, I'm too old, but my daughter should do that, she should not live like this."

It changed how I felt about this part of the world. When I arrived and looked at this beautiful valley, clouds moving through the mountains, orange sunsets over the water and people busy farming and selling produce in town. The truth was these people were poor but not isolated; they knew how people lived elsewhere and wanted to live that way too.

The project moved forward, and we ended up focusing all hotel development in the unused areas where there was significant environmental damage, mainly the two quarries. We created some village 'home' stay areas, walking trails and luxury mountain retreat locations. The landmark we intended to develop was to be like the Eden Project development that used the quarries as botanic gardens under huge domes, similar to the landmark in England. We were to eventually create a food trail throughout the valley utilising restaurants in each location, among other attractions.

Tourism, in many cases, makes the world a better place and westerners must avoid the 'Noble Savage' trait of the 19th century, thinking their primitive ways are romantic to us, while we live in luxury with smartphones and tablets. Developed communities should not look down at other cultures and think of them as majestic in their 'savagery'. They should not be held back so we have an interesting culture for us to visit. It is not our choice to make. Often the simplest solution is just to ask locals what they want. They may want an iPhone but also keep their bee eating traditions.

On the other end of the tourism spectrum from isolation, is the concept of *Overtourism*. Landmarks can act as a significant drawcard that pulls people from all over the world to cram into one small space. Twenty-six million people flock to the small island of Venice every year to experience the landmarks of Saint Mark's Campanile and Piazza San Marco. All businesses that once catered for locals are gone, leaving only souvenir stores and high-priced restaurants behind. It functions more like Disneyland than as a community. Barcelona is experiencing a similar problem, the centre of Paris has been dealing with it for many years, and New York and London are not immune to the overtourism pressure.

Airbnb and other guest-sharing apps have exasperated this problem. Historically, a location would only have enough hotel beds to balance out the low season with the high. It was common for hotels to be full in peak season. In the past, sometimes a whole city would run out of accommodation. Now we have an endless supply of beds. In theory, if tourists are willing to pay enough, every resident can temporarily move out, and a tourist could take their place.

During a major event, like the Olympics, many residents are displaced by visitors. We now no longer have a ceiling on the maximum number of tourists a location can handle; it can go as high as the rental market can absorb. This causes overtourism. The effects of overtourism, of people crowding together, bumping into each other, causing local businesses to disappear in a sea of souvenir stores and high-priced restaurants is saddening, but today with COVID19, it is now a health issue.

The COVID19 crisis has become a time for reflection. We have all been so busy working, travelling, and doing many activities, we have not had time to think about *why*. As our landmarks lie empty and wildlife returns to our natural areas, the time to ask *why* is now. *The Great Landmark Race* is about this *why*. Why our civilisations build monuments to self, our gods, or our corporations; it is about a race to be the tallest, the biggest, to have meaning and to be remembered. It is about seeking attention, acknowledgement, and fame. It is a never-ending race with each civilisation striving to compete with all the others throughout time. It is about inspiration and creation. It is about being great, the greatest places on Earth, and how one day we can all be able to get out and explore them again.

2. The Great Bucket List

"Be not afraid of greatness. Some are born great, some achieve greatness, and others have greatness thrust upon them." William Shakespeare, Twelfth Night

I drafted my first bucket list of landmarks while at the town planning office in Wuhan, China. The term 'bucket list' can mean a list of great places you wish to visit before you kick the bucket. The reference to a bucket means either, a bucket stood on while being hanged, or in William Shakespeare's sense (*Henry IV*, Part II), of being a cross piece of wood held over the shoulders to carry buckets, which was also used in hanging. I have been using this term for a long time and had no idea it was so grim. Regardless, do you have a bucket list of top landmarks you wish to visit before you kick it?

Before COVID19, Wuhan was unknown to the world even though it had a population of eleven million. At the time, I could have never imagined one day the smallest thing in the world, a virus, would deliver fame to Wuhan and not a world standard landmark we were planning. Yet, it was our goal to create an *attraction*, not a *repulsion*.

In the summer of 2006, I arrived in Wuhan directly from a meeting in Zhuhai, southern China, where we were planning the construction of the world's tallest building. Due to flight scheduling problems, I arrived five hours too early to the workshop. Unfortunately, my lack of Mandarin and only knowing the meeting address, coupled with my fear of getting lost, caused me to head straight to the meeting unfashionably four hours too early. The ride to the city planning office was exciting. Being in a city I had never heard of, I crossed the famous Yangtze River, passed one of the largest steelworks in the world that was a kilometre long, and through little villages, hidden behind towering residential blocks.

Once at the office, I was taken to one of the directors' rooms and sat face to face with her for a minute when I realised how challenging the next few hours would be. She did not speak English, and I did not speak Mandarin. It was apparent she did not know what to do with me. Before long, we found a way around the problem. We started to communicate using drawings on a notepad. We pointed at pictures in books and used simple words like *yes*, *no,* and *that* to talk. I discovered she was a collector of tea with jars of all different types around her office. When I showed appreciation of this, she decided to direct me through the hundreds of tea containers, pointing at maps to show me their origin. Between bouts of drinking tea and running to the bathroom, we eventually came around to a discussion of where in the world we most wanted to visit. She explained that she had never left China, and she wanted to know my bucket list.

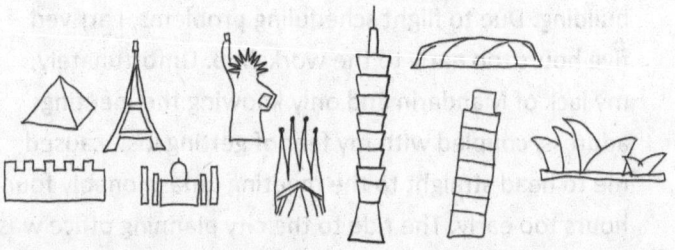

Figure 1: My Top 10 Landmarks.

I started to draw out a series of pictures of the top ten places I thought were the best landmarks in the world (see Figure 1). I started with two triangles, which meant the Pyramids of Giza. Second, I'm not sure if this was to appease her or if it was my legitimate second choice, but I drew two long lines, the top being a square zig zag. The lines represented the Great Wall of China. I placed a tick next to this, as I had been there and the same with the Pyramids. (Was I showing off to a person who had never left her country? Possibly.) The third was another triangle with two curving sides and horizontal lines above the bottom – the Eiffel Tower, another tick. Fourth was a dome on a square with four towers, and this took longer to explain; it was the Taj Mahal, no tick. The list continued with a squiggly drawn hat – Statue of

Liberty. The Sagrada Familia, as I'm a fan of Gaudi. Taipei 101, the tallest building in the world. Uluru, the oldest landform on the oldest landmass in the world. The Leaning Tower of Pisa – a rectangle drawn leaning (it took a while to explain this one, but it received a good laugh, once understood). Finally, I made a drawing of the Sydney Opera House because I'm Australian and had to represent my country and show off with another tick.

The Wuhan List

1. Pyramids of Giza
2. Great Wall of China
3. Eiffel Tower
4. Taj Mahal
5. Statue of Liberty
6. Sagrada Familia
7. Taipei 101
8. Uluru
9. Leaning Tower of Pisa
10. Sydney Opera House

I thought this conversation was just filling in time until the workshop late that afternoon, amongst a craze of hand gestures, interpreters, PowerPoint slides and large sheets of drawings, I had a piece of paper handed to me from an interpreter. It was my top 10 list of drawings, but written across the top was the Chinese characters for Wuhan. I looked around and saw my tea friend looking at me from across the room, nodding.

The interpreter explained she wanted our goal for the project to be a landmark that would be at the top of that list. A landmark that people would most want to visit in the world. She wanted a landmark for Wuhan that would be on everybody's bucket list.

At this point, I wish I had an incredible story to tell you about how we designed the Great Statue of Wuhan, the Great Wuhan Opera house or even the Great Pyramids of Wuhan, but we did not. Through a series of workshops, the project came around to designing the largest building in the world, to rival the Taipei 101 building and to rival our other project in Zhuhai. The size of the building was eventually reduced to just a very tall building today. It was common in this time, especially in China, for cities to all want to have the tallest building in the world, and it was not until the construction of Burj Khalifa in Dubai, in 2010, that Taipei 101 was defeated.

I always felt responsible the project did not go the way it should as we resorted to the old trope of the *tallest building in the world*, which did not eventuate. As urban designers, we should have been able to come up with a concept that could have been on everyone's bucket list. We should have imagined an idea the world would have considered to be *great*.

The role of the urban designer is to develop a vision for a project. A vision should reflect the aspirations of everyone involved. These are the clients with their ambitions, the community and their wants, and the government and their goals. The concept needs to be real, achievable, profitable, and exciting. If it is not exciting or a strong idea, it will not attract attention. Attention also means investment, property sales and leases. Our profession is constrained by planning legislation, budgets and public consultation restrictions with the whole design process a balancing act. A *good* design is a plan that achieves all this; a *great* plan is one that does all this and more.

There are always questions when developing a landmark. For example, we often get pushback from the community, *'Why build a big icon when we have homelessness, unemployment and economic problems? Why should we develop an attraction at all? For whom? Is it just for tourists?'*

Having worked at City Council and prioritised the local community's need over all else, it is difficult to counter these points. In private consulting, we have difficulty raising the aspirations of the client to achieve something truly great, with cost always being an issue. It is also difficult to get governments to think past the next election and even for China to think past their five-year plan. It is because of all these reasons that our world has very few *great* landmarks.

Figure 2: Sydney Opera House.

A great landmark can provide immense value to a location. An interesting example is a report on the monetary value the Sydney Opera House provides to Sydney and Australia. In a report produced by Deloitte in 2013[4], they valued the social asset value of the Opera House to be 4.6 billion dollars. They calculated the value at three levels:

- Economic Contribution: Direct ticket sales contributed through goods and services, and the supply chain benefits into other sectors. Directly attracting tourists to the precinct who spend $775 million in a year visiting Sydney.
- The Audience Value: Based on calculations on how much an Australian would pay for the upkeep of the Sydney Opera House, in tax evaluation of $4.6 billion over the lifetime of the building. It is a value placed on its cultural heritage and identity as a national icon.
- Its Brand: The Opera House brand is ranked second in Australia, just after the brand of 'Australia' itself.

- Digital footprint: Visitors were surveyed to determine the digital value of the building through online sources like Facebook and streaming of festivals with respondents prepared to pay $5.60 per view.

This study highlights the impact a landmark can have on a city, country, and the world. The economic benefits are incredibly high for a successful landmark. Its cultural and community value, as a city and national icon, can be measured to take this into account.

Australia's second-largest export after iron ore is tourism. Tourism is considered an export as it brings money into the country and exports *experiences* to other nations. It provides jobs, cross-cultural exchange and has supply chain benefits from tour bus maintenance to restaurants. Furthermore, it is far less damaging to the environment than iron ore mining.

The factors that make a landmark great has preoccupied my time for over ten years. As an urban designer and researcher, I felt there were exact components that make a landmark successful. I felt our clients, communities and economies needed certainty when we design a landmark that will achieve the goals we set for it. The world has so few *great* landmarks, and people need to disperse more widely around the world, yet designers struggle with creating attractions that can work at an international scale. We have communities on our planet suffering hardship and if a landmark was created, those communities could flourish. I do not just mean economically, the influx in tourism dollars can be used to help protect the environment, can provide social services, better waste recycling, all things tourists value in a destination. The best way to do this is through a landmark attraction, and the best way to design a landmark attraction is to analyse existing landmarks, determine what makes them great in a scientific way, and use the information to design new destinations.

This quest to understand what makes a great landmark began with the Wuhan bucket list and continued when I attempted to revise it.

I first decided to make a master list of the top ten landmarks in the world. I researched online, in the newspaper, and browsed travel guides all titled 'The top 10 landmarks in the world', 'Top 25', or even 'Top 500'.

Taking one of these lists and comparing it to mine, I noticed at number nine was the Iguazu Falls in Argentina. I had never heard of this waterfall. To have a list of the world's greatest landmarks and to have an entry that was unknown to me was perplexing. Was it me? Am I living in a bubble? Or was it the list?

Figure 3: Iguazu falls.

The Iguazu falls are considered a geological wonder of the world. On the border of Argentina and Brazil, the water drops from a height of 82 metres and has a width of 2.7 km, it is wider than both Niagara Falls, and Victoria Falls[5]. The falls look amazing, multi-tiered, crashing down on all sides of a valley (see Figure 3: Iguazu fallsFigure 3). While looking at photos of it I realised that at one time I had it as a Windows desktop wallpaper, this discovery presented me with two choices. Either update my bucket list and book a ticket to Argentina or ignore this list and see if I could find another, with cheaper airfares and landmarks I know. My mistake here was to take the more affordable option. I searched again and found a different list of top fifteen greatest landmarks.

The next article had an entry at number twelve for the Willis Tower in Chicago. Although this building was once the tallest in the world (in 1973), today it is the sixteenth. How can it make it onto a list of 15 greatest landmarks in the world and not even be one of the 15 tallest buildings in the world? And what about Cloud Gate? This large, mirrored, bean-shaped sculpture which distorts the world around it, fantastic for photographing (see Figure 4), is far greater than Willis Tower. The sculpture is located close to the tower in Millennium Park. If they wanted a Chicago entry, this is a far better candidate.

Figure 4: Cloud Gate, Chicago.

I soon concluded that the definition of what is considered *great* was very loose. The search continued until I had reviewed around 30 articles from the internet, news sites and tourism advertising. What became apparent is that although there were many inconsistencies, and no list was identical, there were some landmarks that were consistent. For example, the Eiffel Tower in Paris consistently made the top 10. Still, there were also others, Neuschwanstein Castle, for example, that would be ranked high in some European centric lists and then was absent from other more global lists. After a time, all these *top* rankings were collated into an Excel spreadsheet, to hopefully come up with a singular list where consistencies could rise to the top. The aim was to create a meta-list or super list of top landmarks in the world.

The list ended up being 2,340 entries long.

Whenever a new article gets posted, for example, 'Expedia 2019 top 50 landmarks', I would create a new column and add the ranking to each entry. If the landmark was not yet listed, then a new line was added. Therefore, having 2,340 entries highlight the significant diversity writers, bloggers and voted opinion pieces have when they rank the World's Greatest Landmarks. How *great* is a landmark, then, if it gets added as entry 2,340? For your information, it is the 'World's Largest Artificial Trout' in Adaminaby, Australia. It was added from a list of the World's Great Tourist Attractions, and it was ranked last.

The table is considerably large in landmarks down the side and with rankings across the top. The most exhaustive list was from Lonely Planet in their 'Ultimate Travel List of 500 best places on earth...

ranked'[6] which took longer than a flight to Argentina to collate.

The next step and aim of this exhaustive journey, was to add an aggregate score that averaged all the lists to create a combined list of landmarks. The most consistent entry would appear at the top, and the least consistent would rank at the bottom. What follows is what Expedia polls, Lonely Planet researches and even Kids World Travel.com[7], among others, all believe, in their opinion, to be the top 10 greatest landmarks in the world. This is a list of *opinions*, like a meta-list.

The meta bucket list of most popular great landmarks:

1. Taj Mahal
2. Bayon Temple at Angkor
3. Machu Picchu
4. Eiffel Tower
5. Great Wall of China
6. Pyramids of Giza
7. Sagrada Familia
8. Acropolis
9. Golden Gate Bridge
10. Statue of Liberty

The meta bucket list of most popular landmarks in the world instantly... felt incorrect. Is the Taj Mahal truly the greatest landmark in the world? So, all the entries below it are not as good? I feel the Pyramids of Giza, based on age and its iconic shape, should be ranked higher, above Machu Picchu? The Great Wall of China is very long, is it a landmark? Or is it too big? Maybe a part of it is, for example, at its gateways?

This list of meta-opinions is interesting. It indicates popularity, and popularity is a part of being *great*. But it is not factually, objectively, and definitively, a list of *greatness*.

The issue of opinions is an industry-wide problem. In place design, whether it is architecture, urban design, landscape architecture or town planning, has been painting itself into a corner for many years. The industry listens to opinions all the time. Views from various sources can place the designer as merely another opinion in the mix and less of a leader. When it comes to a decision, a client, a council, or the general public, all opinions get considered when designing. The goal is often to create something that makes everyone happy, and as a result, the design ends up being bland.

The reason for this encouraging of opinions is that design is a split between science and art. A building needs to stand and be functional, and it must also be a place for people to enjoy, love and live their lives. Cities need to do the same and so do landscapes and streets. It is the art side of design that has been co-opted by opinions.

In the past, architects, artists, and designers were so famous they could simply just say, "*I, Le Corbusier, think my idea is best*'" **Or,** "*It's a Picasso, therefore it is* *brilliant"*. The world changed mid last century with Andy Warhol and the move away from modernism to post-modernism. Andy understood that the fame of the artists was more about fame and less about art. Today we see fame as more obviously separate from art or design as we have reality tv stars and Instagram influencers who prove this, by having fame but no other talent. Planners, as a dig at architects, refer to them as starchitects. The era of the famous architects has gone, and it is not about the person at the top so much but about the company. Today many of the famous 'influencers' have retired, and their companies are all owned by the next level of architects that delivered on the famous projects. Today, a list of architectural practices is a list of corporations and not a list of great design people.

All these issues created a gap that is triggering a revolution in the city design industry. It began by doctors when architects were designing hospitals. Evidence-based Medicine has taken over the medical profession, and today an experienced doctor may recommend a treatment based on their years of experience, and have an intern shoot it down based on proven evidence that shows it to be ineffective. The medical profession has moved into an evidence-based approach where treatment is given based on proven research that works.

Evidence-based approaches flowed into place design when architects were designing hospitals and were questioned by their doctor-clients about what evidence proves this design is better than others.

I first encountered this when my company was designing a new hospital in Singapore. Doctors had insisted on an evidence-based approach to design, so the team organised a full-scale mock-up of a hospital room for doctors, nurses, and patients to use and collected data and interviews to analyse patient care.

This approach has developed into an Evidence-Based Design (EBD) approach and has moved into other areas of design. Looking at sites through evidence is revolutionising the design industry and is pushing it further into the field of science. It has given the power back to experts to counter opinions using research and evidence. A graduate designer can now interject and tell the CEO architect that wind movement patterns make his design very windy around the base. In the 1950s, the intern would be advised to shut up, today the CEO listens.

Evidence-Based Design has opened the industry to a suite of new possibilities. We now no longer just judge a landmark based on what people's opinions are but also on what qualities it has that makes it great. We can research and find the real reasons for their greatness, or in some cases, if they are as great as we believe them to be. For example, the Tate Modern in London – is it great because of the building or because of its contents? With this said, opinions do have value in understanding what people like and dislike. We need to listen to the views through the lens of Evidence-Based Design as this method can answer the question of *why*. Why people like a particular landmark, and why people dislike another, is how we become better at landmark design. In this way, we can indeed find and build things that are great rather than just using an acceptance of opinion.

This search for what makes great landmarks, *great*, and why there are winners and why there are losers, is an evidence-based approach by using people's opinions to understand the truth about *why* landmarks are significant. With an Excel list of opinions as a meta bucket list of great landmarks in hand, the next task is to analyse this list to uncover why these landmarks are considered great. Finally, we can make a definitive list of what are the greatest landmarks in the world.

3. Landmarks

"Learn the rules like a pro, so you can break them like an artist." Pablo Picasso

As with all races, there are rules to stop people cheating. In the landmark race, some people bend the rules to claim victory when victory is far from sight. They use words to twist their landmark into victory position. For example, there is *The Tallest Residential Building in the Southern Hemisphere* or the *Largest Ball of Twine in the World, Made by One Man*. If the competition to build the most significant landmark in the world is considered a race, then these twisted definitions of large and tall are in fact, cheating. Often this is done as a marketing spin to give prestige to a landmark that is less deserving of the title *Great*.

To make a clean landmark race with evidenced-based results, we must lay down race rules that are unbiased and make all contestants equal. In assessing a landmark, we first need to define what a landmark is. Also, we need to exclude those that are not landmarks to prevent skewing the results. The definition of a landmark needs to be logical and straightforward to all.

To begin with, the biggest problem with landmarks is that there are two definitions in English. In North American English it is considered,

"a building or other place that is of outstanding historical, aesthetic, or cultural importance, often declared as such and given a special status (landmark designation), ordaining its preservation, by some authorising organisation."[8]

The American definition helps to define *greatness* but its description of, *"a building or other place…"*, is unhelpful as it is too broad.

The most beneficial description comes from the British definition:

"An object or feature of a landscape or town that is easily seen and recognised from a distance, especially one that enables someone to establish their location."[8]

In British English, the meaning is inside the word – something that *marks* the *land*. This definition is far more helpful in defining a landmark. For example, the Great Barrier Reef in Queensland Australia is rated on some lists as one of the world's most significant landmarks. If we analyse it using the following four criteria from the dictionary meaning, the reef fails at being defined as a landmark, and with good reason. If we also test this with the Eiffel Tower, it should succeed.

Object or feature of a landscape or town: The Great Barrier Reef is vast in area and consists of over 3000 individual reefs[9] dotted down the coast. It is not a single object or feature and is not part of a town and not a landscape as it is in the sea. The reef is more of an area or wider locality than a landmark. The Eiffel tower, on the other hand, is a distinct single object or feature.

Easily seen from a distance: The reef is not easily seen from a distance as it is underwater. The Eiffel Tower is easily seen from miles around.

Recognised from a distance: Even underwater, it would be hard to recognise this reef compared to other reefs, especially from a distance. The Eiffel Tower is so distinct in its form, it is easily recognised from a distance.

Establishes a location: The reef is 2300km long and 260km wide[9] and is too big to establish one specific location. The Eiffel Tower establishes its location next to the River Seine in Paris, and is used for navigation throughout the city.

The dictionary definition can be used to include or exclude specific locations. For example, Machu Picchu fits all the above criteria, yet the town of Fez Medina in Morocco is too large. It still *establishes a location*, it can be *recognised at a distance* by its skyline, yet it is not a *contained object or feature* and is not *easily seen* as one singular place.

Alternatively, the Burj Khalifa, the tallest building in the world towers 163 storeys above the city of Dubai. It fits all the criteria due to its triangular form and its height whereas The Address Residence tower in Dubai, the 87th tallest building in the world sits next to other buildings similar in height and shape. It is difficult to distinguish this building without detailed knowledge of cultural architecture. It does not quite achieve the criteria of being recognised from a distance having no overtly distinguishing features as it is similar to its neighbours. It also does not establish a location sufficiently enough to be defined as uniquely Sheikh Mohammed bin Rashid Blvd or Dubai.

To be a great landmark, it must first qualify as a landmark. The more landmark qualities it has, the more it can be recognised, then the greater the landmark is. For example, the Louvre in Paris ranks highly on many opinion lists in the world. It has great contents and has a great glass pyramid entry, but is it a great landmark? Are its contents with the Mona Lisa skewing the buildings greatness?

Therefore, part of the assessment for defining how great a landmark is, needs to have measurement of what landmark qualities it has, and if it is even a landmark in the first place.

This issue arose during the design development of the Alpensia Region for the 2018 Winter Olympics. In 2006 we were designing the site for the 2014 Winter Olympics bid, which was lost, but won for the 2018 Olympics. The region was spread over four valleys with one valley having the existing PyongChang village and our two valleys to be designed with downhill slopes, village centre, toboggin run and a ski jump among other events. The design also included golf courses that can be used in the summer months and acted as cross-country routes in winter.

The main issue was that the location was separated and did not feel as one cohesive location. It was felt that street paving patterns and using the same architecture would unite the valleys. Eventually we made the decision to build the Sky Tower at the top of the ski jump course that sat between the two valleys and could be seen from the other two. The tower became a constant visual landmark for all the region. It helps people navigate and identify the region, both while moving around the villages and watching at home on television. It is a viewing tower with a 360-degree viewing deck with every local Olympic event seen from its height above the mountain. It unites the location in a way paving and brick textures cannot. This solution was a landmark solution in the full sense of the dictionary meaning. Other ideas of flags or sculptures around the resort were considered but the sky tower marked the land like nothing else.

How much a landmark marks the land can help us further distinguish its quality. I developed the following point system to measure how many landmark qualities a building or object has as a way of testing how significant a landmark is based on the British dictionary meaning.

Object or feature of a landscape or town:

0 Points

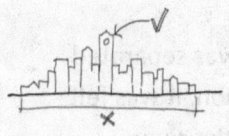

If the landmark is a location, a suburb, or a district, then this is not a landmark. There may be a landmark element in that area, a church or a clocktower, but that does not make the whole location a landmark.

1 Point

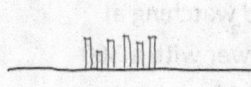

If it is a series of objects, for example, a group of statues on Easter Island, or more tightly grouped like Stonehenge, then this deserves one point.

2 Points

If the objects form part of a whole, like a cathedral with its many spires and alcoves then this receives two points.

3 Points

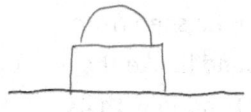

If it is simple in form and appears like one object, often these landmarks are defined as iconic. For example, the Eiffel Tower, Leaning Tower of Pisa with its distinctive lean, or a mosque with a simple dome roof.

Easily seen from a distance:

0 Points

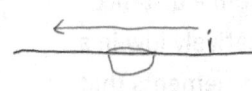

If the landmark is hidden – for example, the Carlsbad Caverns in the United States – then it does not get any points. If it is too large, such as the UNESCO site of the 'Historic Town of Guanajuato and Adjacent Mines' in Mexico, which cannot be seen in its entirety from a distance, it receives no points.

1 Point

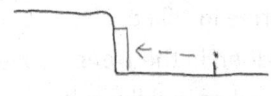

Some landmarks are partially hidden. The Trafalgar Falls in the Dominican Republic is impressive but it can only be seen from one direction.

Landmarks which can only be seen from one location, receive only one point.

2 Points

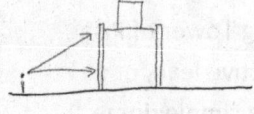

If a landmark can be seen from everywhere around it, like the Tate Modern in London with its tall tower that can be seen from multiple locations, then it receives two points.

Recognised from a distance:

0 Points

If you must be up close (less than ten metres) to see the landmark, then this is not considered 'from a distance'. Also, if it is relatively low in a group of taller elements that obscure it, it also gets zero points.

1 Point

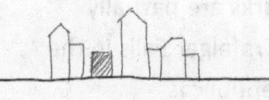

If the landmark can be seen from between ten and one hundred metres away, it gets one point. An example is the Futarasan Shrine in Nikko, Japan. It is hidden in the trees and amongst other buildings, it may earn points in different categories, but it only yields one point here.

2 Points

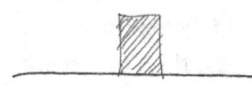

If seen from 100 metres to 750 metres away, and the landmark is still recognisable, this earns it two points. The Bayon Temple at Angkor in Cambodia is seen from a fair distance away, any farther and it gets lost amongst the trees as its height is just 34 metres.

3 Points

For distances greater than 750 metres, three points are given. Big Ben in London is an example of a 96-metre-tall landmark with a distinctive shape that is recognisable from a distance.

Height does govern this category, but also to a lesser degree, so does context. Uluru, the large singular rock in the flat desert of Australia is amazingly distinctive. In contrast, Ko Tapu in Phang Nga Bay, Thailand, a tall rock structure in the ocean (also known as James Bond Island) is surrounded by rock cliffs and mountains and is more difficult to see.

Establishes a location:

0 Points

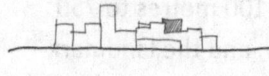

If a landmark does not help you navigate your way, then it earns no points. For example, the whole city of New York together may help you navigate from across the river in New Jersey, but it is useless if you are in Broadway, as the whole city is around you. Individual features help you navigate, not a city as a whole. If it is not easily seen or is made up of too many objects in different locations, then it can't be used for navigation.

1 Point

If it helps people navigate through all areas, then one point is given.

This point system helps us assess what level an object is a landmark. If it receives 9 points, then it is like the Eiffel Tower or Saint Basil's Cathedral in Russia. If it gets below four points like Convento de San José in Spain, hidden and part of a complex, then it may not be considered a landmark. If the score is below three, then it is not a landmark using this system. The Grand Canyon falls into this category as it is too big, and even if some elements of it might be a landmark, the Canyon as a whole is not. The landmark elements can be reviewed separately, for example, the Grand Canyon Skywalk, a glass bridge the loops over the cliff edge makes for a great landmark. (See Figure 5: Grand Canyon Skywalk.)

Figure 5: Grand Canyon Skywalk.

When we apply the point system to the previous meta bucket list of popular landmarks, we get the following top 10 results:

1. Taj Mahal
2. Eiffel Tower
3. Pyramid of Giza
4. Machu Picchu
5. Bayon Temple at Angkor
6. Golden Gate Bridge
7. Statue of Liberty
8. Sagrada Familia
9. Sydney Opera House
10. Acropolis

The Taj Mahal is still number one; the Eiffel Tower has moved up and so has the Pyramid of Giza due to its simple form as a landmark. The Sydney Opera House made it into the list, with the Great Wall of China dropping off to number 21. The wall is still great, but as a landmark, it is too long to be defined as one place. Therefore, it would be difficult to use it for navigation. If you are standing in front of the Great Wall, where specifically along its length are you?

Figure 6: The Great Wall of China.

4. The Race

"Great rivalries don't have to be built on hatred. They're built on respect, on a respect for excellence."
Mike Krzyzewski, American Basketball Coach

People love to compete. Whether it is in sport, business, computer games, or even who is dressed best at a party, there is always some rivalry.

Cities compete too. Every city or town has its rival location. Typical rivalries are as follows:

> Hong Kong versus Singapore
> Los Angeles versus New York
> Beijing versus Shanghai
> Glasgow versus Edinburgh
> Manchester versus Liverpool
> Houston versus Dallas
> Seoul versus Busan
> Melbourne versus Sydney
> London and Paris

There is also the big rivalry between Springfield and Shelbyville, from *The Simpsons*.

If we take Google trends[10] and look at commonly searched terms, we can see London is winning in terms of popularity. So is Hong Kong over Singapore, New York over Los Angeles, Shanghai over Beijing, Seoul over Busan, Glasgow slightly more than Edinburgh, with Manchester, Houston, Seoul, and my cities competitor, Sydney, all beating their rivals.

If we look at these rival cities and their landmarks, for example, London and Paris, we see Big Ben with the Tower Bridge versus The Eiffel Tower and Arc de Triumph. The competition is relatively close when we compare landmarks.

To further understand city rivalry, it is useful to look at China. The country has a categorisation system for cities known as Tiers. Tier 1 belongs to the principal cities that are more populous, technologically advanced, have higher GDP and the most infrastructure. They are the cities of Beijing, Tianjin, Shanghai, Chongqing and Guangzhou. Tier 2 cities are Suzhou, Nanjing, Wuxi adding to a total of 30 cities. Tier 3 has 136 cities with Wuhan being one of them, and there are around 490 cities at Tier 4. This system is not a precise category system, and there are arguments. There are always cities that like to think of themselves as up to the next category.

Global cities are thought of in the same way but without the tier label. Global categorisations systems are reasonably robust, yet numbers get tweaked by changing a GDP cut off amount to add a city into a higher GDP category, or pushing the population up a bit to incorporate a neighbouring city. Seoul and Incheon, is it really all one place? San Francisco and Oakland – that Bay Bridge is long, are you sure you are the same city with a combined population? Definitions aside, Richard Florida, a well-published (and personal idol) city analyst has produced the following list called the Global City Economic Power Index, that ranks world cities.

Rank	City/Metro
1	New York
2	London
3	Tokyo
4	Hong Kong
5	Paris
6	Singapore
7	Los Angeles
8	Seoul
9	Vienna
=10	Stockholm
=10	Toronto
12	Chicago
13	Zurich
=14	Sydney
=14	Helsinki
=16	Dublin
=16	Osaka-Kobe
=18	Boston

=18	Oslo
=18	Beijing
=18	Shanghai

Source: Richard Florida, Citylab[11]

Sydney, my city's rival, is located at equal 14th. Melbourne is not listed. Recently when shopping in Melbourne City, I noticed a sign above a fashion store listing their shops- *'London, Paris, Tokyo, New York, Melbourne.'* It is interesting how my city is listed as one of the top great cities. The absence of Sydney seems suspiciously deliberate. It raises the question: do they have shops everywhere and just tack on the local city? Is there a sign in one of the smallest towns in the world, in Canada[12] with a population of six people that says, *'London, Paris, Tokyo, New York, Tilt Cove'*?

The rivalry between Sydney and Melbourne is a fascinating race of landmarking. There is a clear winner here with Sydney and its harbour, its rugged coastline with open views for kilometres past the heads and out to the Pacific Ocean. Manly Beach up the coast on the left and Bondi Beach on the right. You could stick a three-storey high block of concrete on that harbour, and it would instantly become a landmark. In 1973, Sydney placed an Opera House on it. The expert evaluation report from UNESCO states,

"It stands by itself as one of the indisputable masterpieces of human creativity, not only in the 20th century but in the history of humankind."

The city of Melbourne has on its narrow brown river, the Concert Hall. A round brownish concrete 1980s' building, a bit like a hockey puck. (See Figure 7.) UNESCO has not classified this concert hall. Maybe they have been too busy?

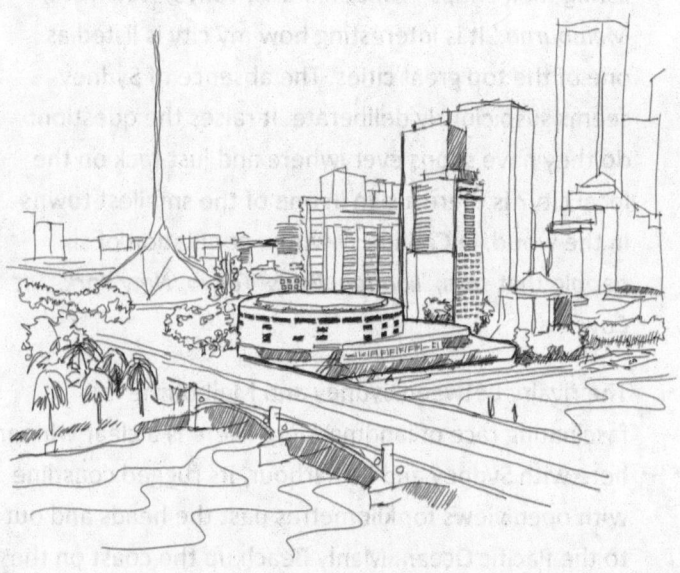

Figure 7: Melbourne Concert Hall in the foreground with the Arts Centre left and Southbank Right.

The Sydney Opera House design comes from the result of an international competition in 1956 that called for, "*the best opera house that can be built*"[13]. Two hundred and thirty-three entries were received from around the world with the judge, Eero Saarinen stating that the winning design *"...concept of an opera house which is capable of becoming one of the great buildings of the world"*[13]. Danish architect Jørn Utzon, was that winner. His modernist concept was for a series of concrete shells, reminiscent of sails on ships are the main feature. The building appears to float out on the Harbour. In 1966 a dispute between Utzon and the State Government caused Utzon to leave Australia. A government-appointed panel continued the work and the design was adjusted to prevent the shells from toppling over. Opera performers complain to this day that the performance space is too cramped due to the shape of the main shell. Initially, it was to cost seven million dollars. It blew out to 102 million dollars and took fifteen years longer to build. It was Peter Hall, the State Government architect, who was passionate about Utzon's design, who followed the vision to deliver the project to its current status. Utzon intended for a timber interior which Hall fought hard to keep, while others thought it was impossible to construct timber on a curving structure. The solution was to get wooden boat builders to help with the construction.

Back in Melbourne, on the 6th of November 1984, the Concert Hall, also known as Hamer Hall, opened in the city[14]. Architect Roy Grounds was also the designer of the Art Centre, an Eiffel Tower-shaped spire mesh located next to it, in 1984, creating an Arts Precinct. The spire was built initially to a height of 115 metres.

At the time, council planning restrictions would not allow any building on the South Bank to be taller than the spire. When the spire needed renovation, it was raised to 162 metres in height which sparked a building boom to reach the new height limit. Today, the state government has pushed through so many tall buildings the council's height controls are virtually obsolete.

Up in Sydney, the Harbour Bridge was built in 1932, before all these other landmarks. A steel arched engineering marvel, it crosses the narrowest point from Sydney City to Milsons Point. (See Figure 8.) Two towers were placed at each end for aesthetic purposes and to deter people referring to it as *the coat hanger*. Sydney also has Sydney Tower. It looks like the Space Needle in Seattle, the CN Tower in Toronto and the Sky Tower in Auckland. It also resembles the Canton Tower, Kuala Lumpur Tower, Milad Tower in Iran, and… the list goes on. You can see my point how it lacks originality as a landmark. Cities are so desperate to compete they often copy each other's successes.

Figure 8: Sydney Harbour Bridge.

In the competition between the two cities, Sydney beats Melbourne. As a *Melbournian,* this pains me to admit. Sydney is a landmark city, Melbourne is not. In 1978, five years after the construction of the Sydney Opera House, Melbourne ran a competition for the site opposite the Arts Centre on the Yarra River, now occupied by Federation Square.

The entries went on display at the public records office in 2011, and it was a fantastic display of what is defined in Australian slang as a 'piss-take' (meaning teasing or mocking someone). Yet there is no denying that if any of them were built, Melbourne would be put on the world stage.

One interesting entry was the architectural construction of a giant hand, pointing up to the sky, with its thumb out in what is now known as the *loser* gesture. It was to be constructed of steel and was to weather to a reddish-brown colour. The thumb to the side would be a restaurant poking out, and the upward-pointing finger would have its nail, a glass viewing deck, higher than everything else in the city. Written on the entry is, *"... it symbolises nothing specifically, but many things generally. Its ultimate worth lies in its enduring gravity, offset with a touch of whimsy."*[15]

Another entry is of a giant letter 'M'. Again, taller than all other buildings in the city, it would be hollow and made of tubular steel with blue reflective glass. The top would have restaurants and a commercial space would be at its base. The entry suggests, *"The hollow shapes of the M will enclose some of the most spectacular man-made spaces on earth."* Again, it is merely a giant 'M.'

The next entry represents the stars on the Australian flag known as the Southern Cross. I guess it hoped to win by appealing to a sense of patriotism. This submission has triangular tent-like structures arranged in the shape of the stars. One star, surrounded by fountains, has a giant tube out of the top of it with a round UFO viewing structure at its summit, it looks like it would be around 50 storeys high. If Seattle's Space Needle can do it, I guess Melbourne can too.

One sketch shows two giant, Statue of Liberty sized kangaroos wearing boxing gloves. One is on the north bank facing the city with the other on the south bank facing south. Both back each other with their tails joined to form a bridge over the river. The entrances to the bridge are through the space between its long feet, about where its genitals would be. A central feature of the design is the two gigantic dollar signs held up by the kangaroos, like the Statue of Liberty's torch.

Kangaroos were prevalent in this competition. Another entry had a kangaroo as a singular statue with a baby joey in her pouch. A visitor would be able to climb up inside her tail into an internal sphere with the galaxy and stars shown inside like a planetarium. The top was to be a viewing tower, with the ears pivoting out of the way to see the sky at night.

The *Yarra Croco(dile)* entry is a giant Chinese-type dragon, shaped a bit like a crocodile. The structure was made of green and gold triangulated steel and concrete with its mouth open to the City and its tail bent up to form a tower and viewing deck. The structure is all taller than the city with its tail about twice the height of the existing city buildings.

The entry states, *"Croco is… [to fit] …extremely naturally into the landscape and rises to the dominating construction of the town. Head and back of Croco will give the impression of a green, hilly ridge of land overlooking its surroundings."*[15] I wonder if anyone thought to mention crocodiles are indigenous to the north of the country and not to Melbourne.

Some of the designs were architecturally very interesting; some were of tall towers and others of retro-future type curving concrete. A fascinating design was a glass, three-sided pyramid, many storeys high, like the entrance to the Louvre which was built ten years later. The entry that pushes the boundary and may have even caused the cancellation of the competition is titled, *"Melbourne's Monumental Mammaries"*. Put simply; it is two gigantic mounded female breasts of ten storeys in height. Pink and strangely, perfectly circular, the nipples pinpoint the centre. The entry goes on to show how printing them on t-shirts would be a good marketing opportunity.

Consequently, the space above the rail lines remained empty until 2002 when what is now known as Federation Square was built. A low-rise series of buildings surrounding an organic triangulated public plaza. (See Figure 9: The current buildings at Federation Square.) Melbournians love the Square as a functional space. In 2018 there was a plan to remove the Aboriginal Centre from the site and build a glass Apple Store in its place. More than 2,000 submissions opposing the concept, including my own, were received and the idea was shelved.

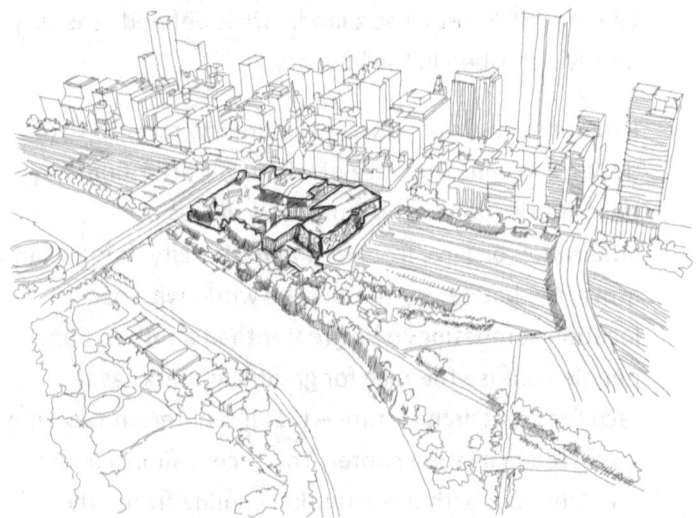

Figure 9: The current buildings at Federation Square.

Urban designers are employed by governments and property developers to produce a concept design for a location. Once an urban designer has completed their role, it is up to planners, architects and landscape architects to continue the project through. An essential component of urban design is to create a *vision* for the project. The aim of a visioning exercise can be to create a landmark that attracts tourists. It could be to gain buyer's attention to boost property sales, to help build civic pride, or in smaller locations, to assist in placemaking (giving a place identity). It could be to simply help people find their way through a district (wayfinding). City councils will often designate a location for future landmarks or have policies to prevent new structures dominating existing landmarks[16]. Yet what a landmark is defined as is very poorly described in the industry.

Urban designers are always required to *race,* so their design can win. The prize of winning is attention may be in tourist dollars, high property values or admiration or envy from its competing city. It is like an arms race happening around the world with each location competing to be greater than another. Some people confuse the race for great landmarks as the race for great architecture – that is a different race and discussed in a later chapter. This race is simply a race for attention, with the attention coming from other cities, tourists, large corporations and, in some cases, from the gods.

What a location needs is a *great* landmark that attracts attention from all over the world, but what is defined as *great* and not just *good*, is what we are searching for here. There is a part of me that questions if the goal is just to attract attention, then *Melbourne's Monumental Mammaries* would gain a great deal of fame if built. Then again, it would be quite sexist and attract negative attention. On second thought... maybe the kangaroos would be better.

5. The Race for Tall

"I don't know what London's coming to - the higher the buildings the lower the morals." Noël Coward, Collected Sketches and Lyrics[17]

Throughout history, civilisations have always strived for greatness, and with landmarks, superiority has often meant tall. The need to create something as tall as a mountain gives a feeling of conquering nature with the view down to the people below giving a sense of superiority. The race for the tallest structure in the world has been run since the first caveman put two stones on top of each other, then stood on them.

It has never been a clean contest. Even Donald Trump, hours after the fall of the World Trade Center, boasted how his building was now the tallest in downtown Manhattan[18]. His building, 40 Wall Street, ranks number 23 in New York, and even with his definition of 'downtown', 70 Pine Street is just nearby and is eight metres taller.

There are also arguments based on how the location is defined. The use of qualifiers such as in which hemisphere, continent, country or state the landmark dominates is often used. Height is the most problematic, with some arguing it is only about storeys. Others claim it is about distance while some include aerials and spires while others do not.

The Council of Tall Buildings and Urban Habitat (CTBUH) defines height as the level of the lowest, significant, open-air, pedestrian entrance to one of three categories[19]:

- Height to its architectural top
- Height to the highest occupied floor
- Height to the tip of the building

The Council also admits that the definition is subjective, not only on height, but on the meaning of 'building'. Regardless, they have created a classification to tightly define the size of a building based on specific parameters. At least these rules make their measurements comparable to each other, whether we agree or not.

After reviewing all the definitions of what is a building and what is height, I feel it is best to ignore all the parameters and simply measure any structure by whatever is tallest in the air. This definition is regardless of guy-cables, habitable rooms, and aerials - if it is in the air, it is measured. This inclusive definition still needs to be controlled by the description of a landmark from the previous chapters. In summary, it must be on land; we do not measure oil rigging platforms height above the ocean floor (they would win everything by the way). With this determination, the first known landmark dates from around ten thousand years ago.

8000 BCE-4000 BCE: Tower of Jericho, 7 metres

The lack of historic data places the Tower of Jericho as the first tallest landmark in the world. John Garstang discovered it around the 1930s and gave it its biblically-inspired name. He believed the landmark was part of the Wall of Jericho as described in the *Bible* and dated it around 1400 BCE. It was Kathleen Kenyon, a fascinating British archaeologist in the 1950s who discovered the tower was far older, from around 8000 BCE. She dated the building at about 4000 years older than the biblical age of Earth.

The tower was conical in shape, nine metres in diameter and seven metres in height. It formed part of a city wall that was used for defence. It seems humans first steps at creating landmarks were not for distinction but protection.

It is unusual to place this stronghold as the first winner of the tallest landmark when it was only around two storeys high. It wins the race at this point simply because it is the highest and oldest structure that we have evidence of today and the lack of competition makes this landmark the winner, and it held the title for 4000 years.

4000 BCE-2648 BCE: Anu Ziggurat, 13 metres

One thousand years before Stone Henge and nine metres taller, the Anu Ziggurat was constructed in the forests of Iraq. The region saw the development of large civilisations as the land was fertile, rich with food, water, wood and wildlife for hunting[20]. Unlike elsewhere in the world, the easy supply of food and materials meant the people had ample free time to devote to construction, improving farming (creating even more free time) and animal rearing instead of hunting.

The civilisation grew, followed by overpopulation which prompted more tree removal for farming and put pressure on water supply. Over time, this once, green land turned slowly into a desert.

Figure 10: Anu Ziggurat.

The Anu Ziggurat was a temple, and today it sits upon a hill in a wind-blown desert appearing as a ruin with

nothing more than foundations and partial walls uncovered by archaeologists. It is visible for kilometres, and was initially shaped as a half-height cube, measuring 17.5 by 22.3 metres with a height of over 14 metres. Surprisingly, it would look in place in virtually any city in the world, as it resembles an office building from the 1950s with fewer windows. (See Figure 10.) It is astonishing that 6000 years ago, a building could be constructed that is similar in shape and form to those we see today. It is around four to five storeys high with doors and window openings, the ground floor is taller, like an office building foyer, and the upper floor windows are smaller. The roof was thin, similar to buildings today due to its use of wood for support. Inside were numerous chambers, two stairways with one being unfinished at the northern end. The rooms contained bookshelves, and archaeologists found pivot stones which implied the use of doors. There were also altars indicating religious use. The surfaces were fire stained signifying it may have burnt down to its foundations.

Dr Senta German indicated the building had a system of plumbing, *"Most interestingly, a system of shallow bitumen-coated conduits were discovered. These ran from the southeast and southwest of the terrace edges and entered the temple through the southeast and southwest doors. Archaeologists conjecture that liquids would have flowed from the terrace to collect in a pit in the centre hall of the temple."*[21]

The Anu Ziggurat is a remarkable piece of architecture for its time and indicates that humans are just as intelligent today as they were 6000 years ago. Today we have far more examples for us to build from whereas they had to invent everything themselves. Therefore, it begs the question, were they more intelligent than us?

2648 BCE-2610 BCE: Step Pyramid of Djoser, 62.6 metres

Djoser was the first king from the third dynasty of Egypt. His highest advisor felt that the king deserved more than the traditional Mastaba (a square, flat-roofed structure) by building a series of six of them on top of one another with each step smaller than the last. Through this feat, he invented the first-ever stepped pyramid. Approximately the height of an eighteen-storey building, it contains 5.5 kilometres of tunnels, thirteen fake doorways and one real entrance. It had a 40-metre-wide trench surrounding the complex with thirteen false access routes to discourage unwanted visitors. A temple also lies on the north side of the pyramid along with a statue of the king[22].

The pyramid is located only fourteen kilometres from the Great Pyramid of Giza and is part of the broader UNESCO World Heritage area. It stood as the tallest known building in the world for 38 years.

2610 BCE-2605 BCE: Meidum Pyramid, 93.5 metres

The Meidum Pyramid took over the race for tallest in 2610 BCE. It was a step pyramid built by the ruler Snofru before he was 15 years of age, yet it was abandoned as a project as Snofru decided to develop in a better neighbourhood 40 kilometres to the north. After overseeing the construction of two more pyramids in the new location, he returned to finish his work on the Meidum Pyramid, making it a *true*, rather than *stepped* pyramid in shape. Snofru was one of the most productive pyramid developers in history. Today the pyramid appears with three steps surrounded by rubble. Researchers assumed the pyramid had collapsed under the weight of the additional stone to smooth out the steps during construction, yet it now appears it collapsed at a much later date[23].

2605 BCE-2600 BCE: Bent Pyramid of Dahshur, 101 metres

Snofru's second pyramid project was the Bent Pyramid of Dahshur. As you can tell by its name, the project also had some problems. The pyramid began a lot smaller and at an angle of 60 degrees. During initial construction, structural issues started to appear, and the base increased in size, and the angle changed to 54 degrees. One third of the way through the project, fearing the pyramid would collapse under its new, greater weight, the angle was reduced to 43 degrees.

This change in direction gave the pyramid its modern name of Bent Pyramid[24]. (See Figure 11.)

Figure 11: The Bent Pyramid of Dahshur was built at 54 degrees and then changed to 43 degrees halfway up to prevent its collapse.

The Bent Pyramid is an excellent example of trial and error. It is through error the pyramid ended up being so big, as its size had to be increased to support its weight. With the myth of pyramids being so perfect that they would have to have been built by aliens, the Bent Pyramid is a fine example of, *"We are human, and we screw up."*

2600 BCE-2570 BCE: Red Pyramid of Dahshur, 105 metres

Learning from this experience, Snofru's new project, the Red Pyramid, was built at the revised angle of 43 degrees. Inscribed at the base of the pyramid is a date the cornerstone was laid. Markings on the stone indicate the date to be the 15th cattle count of Snofru's reign. As cattle counts occurred at irregular intervals, this identifies Snofru's age as being anywhere between

15 and 30 years old[25]. Thirty courses higher, another stone indicates the date to be between 3 to 4 years later, giving an indication it took around 20 years for the pyramid to be built[26].

Snofu's Red Pyramid reined as the tallest structure for thirty years, beating his previous pyramids which reigned for only five years each. His era saw the most prolific building of pyramids in history. It is marvellous that 4,600 years ago, we have a record of how the design of the pyramids developed over time. The failures and abandonment of the Meidum Pyramid, the lessons learnt on the Bent Pyramid and their final success on the Red Pyramid. It is a relatable, human story of experimentation, failure, and success. The most enjoyable part is the effort to go back to the first pyramid and try to fix the mistakes learnt from the next two. The ancient Egyptians built a pyramid, screwed it up, and then went back later to cover their mistakes. Amazing.

2570 BCE-1221CE: Great Pyramid of Giza, 146 metres

The winner of tallest landmark for the most prolonged period (excluding the arguable Tower of Jericho) is the Great Pyramid of Giza, which held the record for 3,791 years and deserving of the prefix 'Great'. It is the last remaining Wonder of the Ancient World and an honorary candidate in the New Seven Wonders of the world. A title voted on by 100 million people in 2007.

The Great Pyramid of Giza stands as the tallest of three large pyramids, along with other smaller secondary pyramids. It is a massive monument surrounded by tombs and the Sphinx of Giza, a large half-pharaoh, half-lion statue. These ancient artefacts are on either side of the River Nile which flows through a green valley, with rich soil and abundant animal and plant life. Over hundreds of thousands of years, the Nile River has washed through the desert creating this valley, like a serpent slithering through the sand. On either side lies the open desert with dunes that shift in the wind. In most pictures of the Great Pyramid of Giza, we see desert surrounding the landmark because most people enter the site from the same direction. If visitors were to turn around at this photo point, they would see cliff edges and the city of Cairo surrounding the Nile River in the valley below. The pyramids are part of a city and not lost alone in the desert. Its height, at the top of the cliffs, adds to their dominance on the skyline. The Great Pyramid of Giza is an impressive 146 metres high and 2.5 million cubic metres in volume.

Its brilliance not only comes from its height and size but from its perfection. Since being built 3,500 years ago, the story of its construction has eroded, creating space for guesswork and speculation. Some feel that a significant landmark could not be built by 'ignorant, ancient people' and would have to be made by those more 'superior' than themselves.

So, who built the Pyramid of Giza? A popular conspiracy theory is that aliens built it. An interesting coincidence is that the speed of light is 299,792,458 metres per second and the Great Pyramid is on the geographic co-ordinate of 29.9792458°N this means aliens must have built it. A problem with this theory is the city of Ningbo in China is built on this parallel. Did aliens construct it too? Houston in the United States, Cornwells Market in Florida, the town of Sidi Boulfdayel on the Moroccan Coast or even the city of Saharanpur in India are all built on this same line meaning they might be made by aliens too? From this, it assumes aliens were looking at the world the same way up as us. Otherwise, the pyramids should have been built in the southern parallel, possibly in the town of Red Rock, Australia, La Serena in Chile, or at the Vanderkloof Holiday Resort in South Africa, all on the same, speed of light parallel. Not to mention that the aliens use metres to measure this too. Sarcasm aside, none of these locations have a conspiracy theory based on them because they are not considered important enough.

Another argument that aliens built the pyramids is based on the idea the blocks would be too heavy to lift. Archaeologists have found evidence of a ramp and post holes on the stones indicating they were pulled from both the back and the front. Proof of this was also found in the quarry where the stones were mined[27].

Archaeologist Mark Lehner wondered at first if aliens had inspired its construction in an interview on PBS,

"I first went to Egypt in 1972 and ended up living there 13 years. I was imbued with ideas of Atlantis and Edgar Cayce and so on. So I went over, starting from that point of view, but everything I saw told me, day by day, year by year, that they were very human and the marks of humanity are everywhere on them."[28]

Another commonly held misbelief is the idea that slaves built the pyramids. Evidence and records show they were constructed by paid labourers who were allowed sick leave and time off to tend crops. This misbelief has its root in the *Bible*, Exodus 1:11, which states that the pharaohs enslaved the Israelites. Yet, Amihai Mazar, professor at the Institute of Archaeology at the Hebrew University of Jerusalem, explains, *"No Jews built the pyramids because Jews didn't exist at the period when the pyramids were built."*[27]

Archaeologists did find that workers on the pyramids lived a short life with many dying of broken bones and injuries suffered during construction.

Theories, conspiracy or otherwise, get linked to famous landmarks while the mundane get ignored. It would be interesting to measure the number of conspiracies a landmark has, compared with its fame, to see if there is a direct correlation.

Landmarks are built to attract attention. The Pyramid of Giza was created to draw attention from the gods to serve them in the afterlife. Other attention it gains, whether in conspiracies or billions in tourism revenue, are all just a by-product of a monument to a deceased ruler.

1221-1311: Old St Paul's Cathedral, 149 metres

Old St Pauls Cathedral, London, was next in the race for tallest structure on Earth and displaced the Great Pyramid of Giza for the title. This monument to god was built to reach the sky and heaven. Gone are the tombs of the dead; this was now the era of churches. Monuments to god were constructed all over Europe, each aiming for greatness in celebration to each civilisation's god.

Construction began on the cathedral in 1087 and it took over 200 years to complete. It was the longest church in the world with some of the finest stained-glass windows. It stood until 1666 as it was undergoing restoration works by Sir Christopher Wren when it was destroyed in the Great Fire of London.

Susan Abernethy wrote in Medievalists.net[29],

"A young student from Westminster School, William Taswell, walked to the cathedral on Wednesday after the fire was spent and found the ground so hot it nearly burned through his shoes. The entire building

was in complete shambles except for the high altar at the east end which was nearly intact. Parts of the building were still burning, smoking or smouldering. The bells were melted. There was a hole where the crypt was with the bookseller's papers still afire. When the roof had collapsed, it had broken effigies and monuments and cracked open tombs and coffins. Bones and corpses were exposed and scattered. The corpse of Robert Braybrooke, a Bishop of London who had died in 1404 was uncovered and found to be perfectly complete and undamaged."

1311-1548: Lincoln Cathedral, 159.7 metres

Before the destruction of Old St Pauls Cathedral, the town of Lincoln, in the East Midlands, challenged the capital to be taller. The cathedral stood for 238 years until its spire collapsed in 1548. It was the tallest church to hold the title of the tallest structure in the world. All other churches to follow never reached its grand height of 159 metres and it would not be until the construction of the Washington Monument in 1884 before its record would be broken.

The Cathedral took one hundred years to build and is still standing today without its central spire. (See Figure 12.)

Figure 12: Lincoln Cathedral with its fallen spire shown greyed out.

1549-1569 and 1573-1647: St Mary's Church, 151 metres

The collapse of the Lincoln Cathedral put St Mary's Church in Germany, which stood in second place since its construction in 1298, up into first place as the tallest structure. The next cathedral triumphed in 1569 by two metres, yet St Mary's won it back when the other tower also collapsed. At this point, the race was less about reaching higher than others and more about being last landmark standing. In 1647, as if god wanted to topple St Marys from her persistent first-place position, lightning struck the spire crumbling it to the ground. It stood tallest for a total of 94 years, over two time periods.

1569-1573: Cathedral of Saint Peter of Beauvais, 153 metres

The cathedral in Beauvais, France, overtook St Mary's when its newly constructed central tower was built two metres higher only to collapse four years later. The building was initially built in 1272 with additions worked into the cathedral throughout its history. The collapse of the spire put to rest any tinkering to the design, and little has changed since.

Figure 13: Strasbourg Cathedral.

1647-1874: Strasbourg Cathedral, 142 metres

Once the fates sealed off St Mary's, St Peters, Lincoln and Old St Pauls all dropping them from the sky, the next in line was the German Strasbourg Cathedral. First constructed in 1439 it was smaller than the Great Pyramid of Giza. Yet, the height of the great pyramid at this time was three metres less due to erosion, granting Strasbourg the gold medal for tallest, by default. In 1874 it was surpassed but the next in the race. Its loss was not due to collapse, lightning strike or war as it still stands today at this grand height. It is now the sixth-tallest church in the world and the highest existing structure built entirely in the Middle Ages. (See Figure 13.)

1874-1876: Church of Saint Nicholas, 147 metres

The Church of Saint Nicholas in Hamburg pushed the race back up in height again, in 1874, by renovating the original building of 1189. The new spire was five metres higher than the previous entry.

During World War II the clearly visible tower served as a wayfinding landmark for the allied bombers, and in 1943 the church was heavily bombed.

In a strange twist in the era of churches, the church was destroyed with the remains demolished, yet its spire survives to present today. With so many Cathedrals dropping out of the race due to collapsing spires, Saint Nicholas Church achieved the exact opposite.

1876-1880: Rouen Cathedral, 151 metres

Another lightning strike hit the wooden spire to the Rouen Cathedral in France, burning it to the ground. Reconstruction of the new spire pushed the building to four metres higher than Saint Nicholas, and it held the record for four years.

1880-1884: Cologne Cathedral, 157 metres

Cologne Cathedral was the last monument to god to win the race for the tallest, and marks the end of the era of churches. It did not reach higher than the Lincoln Cathedral (1311-1549) but still stands today as Germany's most visited landmark even after surviving fourteen bombings during World War II.

1884-1889: Washington Monument, 169 metres

The Washington Monument was designed to be 600 feet (182 metres) in height, but the design of 555 feet and 5⅛ inches was settled on to make it more in proportion with its colonnade base that was never constructed.

One comment on the Constitution Center website states, *"There is also a lesser known Martha Washington monument, which consists of a 555 foot hole in the ground."*[30] For a moment, I thought to look for it on Google Earth before realising the joke was a dig at the monument's penis shape.

The monument is a square obelisk structure, firstly designed by architect Robert Mills to have a circular roman styled colonnade building around its base. Construction began in 1833 with the Catholic Pope donating a cornerstone for the structure, which angered the anti-Catholic Know-Nothing Party. In retaliation, the Party stacked the privately run National Monument Society board causing Congress to cut off funding for five years until the group departed. In 1884, the Army Core of Engineers took over the project and modified the ornate design to be the simple, vertical, phallic design that exists today.

In 1963, the monument was the backdrop to Martin Luther King Junior's famous 'I have a dream' speech. It has also played a role in many movies as its simplicity is perfect at establishing Washington DC as the centre of American political power in only a few movie frames. It has been under attack by aliens and terrorists, while in the background of thrillers and mysteries.

Urban design analysis of the structure reveals it aligns perfectly with the United States Capitol Building and the Lincoln Memorial on the east-west axis. Yet it is misaligned with the White House and the Thomas Jefferson Memorial on the north-east by 390 feet (118.9 metres). This is due to the ground being too unstable to support the monument in this location. (See Figure 14.)

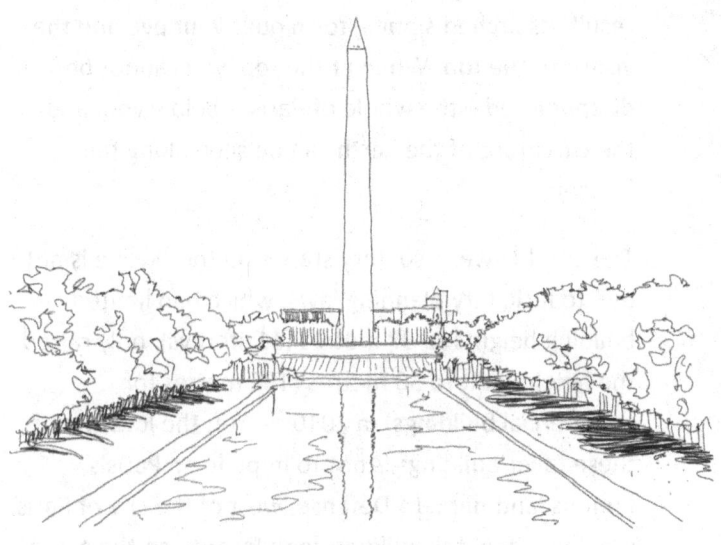

Figure 14: The Washington Monument.

1889-1929: Eiffel Tower, 300 metres

Is the Eiffel Tower the world's greatest landmark? It was the tallest for only 40 years. It is the most visited paid attraction in the world. It is the most copied, with Tokyo Tower, Blackpool Tower and the towers in Las Vegas and Macau, to name only a few. It has the uniqueness of the Washington Monument by being instantly recognisable due to its shape and form, despite the copies. It truly marks the land as a useful landmark should. Nothing is more French. If we receive a postcard from Paris, we expect it to be on the front. When I did a Google image search of Paris, 90 out of the first 100 images are of the Tower, the few that are not, are actually taken from the Tower of the view. A search of the word 'France' yields a similar result. Its arched sloping form pulls your eye and the visitor to the top. When at the top, you cannot be disappointed – the whole of Paris is below you, and the curvature of the Earth can be seen along the horizon.

The Eiffel Tower's solitary stance on the skyline is not due to luck. City planning laws, which had limited building heights to 37 metres (11 storeys), only raised the height limit to 50 metres (180 metres for commercial buildings) in 2010[31]. Yet, the location of these taller buildings is not to impede on Paris's famous landmark. La Défense, west of the city of Paris, is a dedicated, tall building zone located on the axis of the Arc de Triumph and centred around the modern version of the Arc- the Grande Arche de la Défense. It was developed as an expansion area to provide the space needed for the city to compete internationally without overshadowing and challenging the Eiffel Tower. London has a similar location known as Canary Wharf.

1929-1931: Chrysler Building, 318 metres

The Chrysler Building was victorious for only two years. It cost 50 cents, back in 1931, to visit the observation deck which closed in 1945 and is now occupied by a private company. The Art Deco roof tower with its interlaced arcing structure in decorative triangular patterns is reminiscent of the Statue of Liberty's crown. Behind the structure is a hidden apartment which Walter P. Chrysler had boasted was the highest toilet in Manhattan[32].

Above this apartment, author Moses Gates of the book, *Hidden Cities: Travels to the Secret Corners of the World's Great Metropolises,* climbed inside the structure and revealed in a video, *"...you think of the Chrysler Building as Art Deco, shiny, chrome, with metal everywhere. But inside it's all reinforced concrete. You never would have thought it. I expected shiny silver beams holding up the spire."*[33]

At its topmost point, is an antenna spire at the height of 282 metres to its ultimate height of 318 metres.

1931-1954: Empire State Building, 381 metres

The Empire State Building is one of the most famous buildings in the world. It has attracted significant attention based on its height. The giant gorilla, King Kong, could not get enough of it in the movies. Tom Hanks met up with Meg Ryan there in the film, *Sleepless in Seattle*. The building has appeared as a supporting actor in the same way the Washington Monument has, but this time it describes the location as New York City.

As discovered with the Great Pyramid of Giza, great landmarks attract stories and speculation. It was believed that the top of the Empire State Building had a zeppelin docking station. Imagine blimps docking in a steampunk vision of the future. In truth, there is a 200-foot mooring mast that was for docking airships, but it was found that the structure did not account for the wind and it would rip off the top of the building if it were used for anchoring.

The building, unfortunately, attracts tragedy as well as fame. Around 36 people have jumped to the street below from the 86th-floor outdoor observation deck.

For many reasons, one of the most tragic stories is of Evelyn McHale who became well known after *Life Magazine*, on May the 12th, 1947, published a photo of her titled, *'The most beautiful suicide'*. She can be seen in the photo laying as if relaxing on a soft couch, shoes off, feet crossed, one hand raised to her face and the other relaxed over her head. Around her is the crushed wreckage of a parked United Nations Assembly Cadillac appearing like she is sunk into a padded sofa; she seems to be asleep. The note she left behind read,

"I don't want anyone in or out of my family to see any part of me. Could you destroy my body by cremation? I beg of you and my family – don't have any service for me or remembrance for me. My fiancé asked me to marry him in June. I don't think I would make a good wife for anybody. He is much better off without me. Tell my father, I have too many of my mother's tendencies."[34]

The Empire State Building lost the title as the tallest structure in the world in 1954 and plans for the World Trade Centers twin towers, completed in 1970, took away its title of the tallest building as well. Of course, it regained the title of tallest in New York (Willis Tower in Chicago was taller) after the September 11th 2001 disaster when the twin towers collapsed due to a terrorist attack. Its title as the tallest building in New York was lost again to the One World Trade Center in 2014.

1954-1956: Griffin Television Tower, 480 metres

The Griffin Television Tower ended the era of tall buildings (for now) by being constructed to transmit signals as far as possible in the American State of Oklahoma. It was a steel mast with guy-wires stretching out around it to keep it in place. KWTV General Manager, Jack DeLier said in an interview, *"The higher the tower, the more viewers we got."* The tv star, Johnny Carson, was at its dedication, and Vera Ellen, a famous dancer at the time, took the elevator to the 420-metre-high platform and danced to celebrate[35].

With the change of signal from analogue to digital, the tower was decommissioned in 2014, and a scrap metal company was tasked with taking it down to be recycled.

1956-1959: KOBR-TV Tower, 490 metres

Fame escaped this relatively unknown structure. Breaking the record of the world's tallest tower in 1956, in New Mexico, it was constructed similar to the Griffin Tower, but it was knocked down in a storm in 1960.

1959-1960: WGME TV Tower, 495 metres

This tower was built in Maine, and still stands today.

1960-1962: KFVS TV Mast, 511 meters

The American State of Missouri had the tallest tower in 1960 and was so tall it could broadcast to portions of the states of Illinois, Kentucky, Tennessee, and Arkansas.

1962-1963: WTVM/WRBL-TV & WVRK-FM Tower, 533 metres

This tower held the record for around a year. Currently, it does not even have the record for the tallest tower in its American State of Georgia.

1963-1974 and 1991 to 2009: KVLY-TV Mast, 628 metres

The KVLY-TV mast, similar to what happened in the era of churches, was the tallest for two periods in the '60s and '90s and still stands today as the 4th tallest structure in the world, the tallest structure in the Americas, and tallest broadcasting mast in the world. It was succeeded by the following entry, which, when collapsed, was reinstated as the tallest structure again from 1991 to 2009.

1974-1991: Warsaw Radio Mast, 646 metres

Located near the town of Gabin, Poland, this mast stood for 17 years before it collapsed in 1991. A report for 99 Percent Invisible stated,

"An investigating committee determined that blame lay with Mostostal Zabrze, the company which built and maintained the mast. The construction coordinator and the division chief were found liable for the collapse, and both were sentenced to two years in prison."[36]

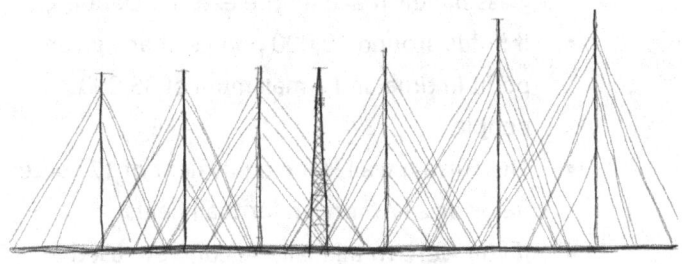

Figure 15: The Television towers height comparison. Left to right- Griffin Television Tower, KOBR-TV Tower, WGME-TV Tower, KFVS TV Mast, WTVM Tower, KVLY-TV Mast, Warsaw Radio Mast.

2009-Today: Burj Khalifa, 829 metres

At the time of writing this the Burj Khalifa, Dubai, United Arab Emirates, is the tallest building and structure in the world. It stands at 829 metres (2,716 feet) high. It has 163 storeys above ground and only one level below. The project cost 1.5 billion dollars. It holds the world record for tallest free-standing building, highest occupied floor, the highest number of storeys, elevator with the longest travel distance, and tallest service elevator. It has the world's second-highest swimming pool, located on the 76th floor. (The world's highest swimming pool is on the 118th floor of Ritz-Carlton Hotel in the International Commerce Centre, Hong Kong)[37].

Some other head-spinning statistics are as follows[38]:

- It took 22 million human hours to build the tower.
- Approximately 26,000 individually hand-cut glass panels make up the exterior cladding.
- It holds around 10,000 people at any given point in time and a maximum of 35,000 people.
- The curtain wall is the equivalent of 17 soccer fields or 25 American football fields.
- If you were to take all the concrete used in Burj Khalifa and lay a sidewalk, it would be 2,065 kilometres (1,283 miles) long.
- The very tip of the spire of Burj Khalifa can be seen from up to 95 kilometres away.
- Skidmore, Owings and Merrill created close to 4,000 drawings when designing Burj Khalifa; when the building was on site, close to 10 times more drawings were produced.

The Burj Khalifa's promotional website expresses the real desire of the Burj Khalifa's stakeholders, developers, state officials and investors, and their intention to win the race for the tallest landmark. The project's vision is as follows.

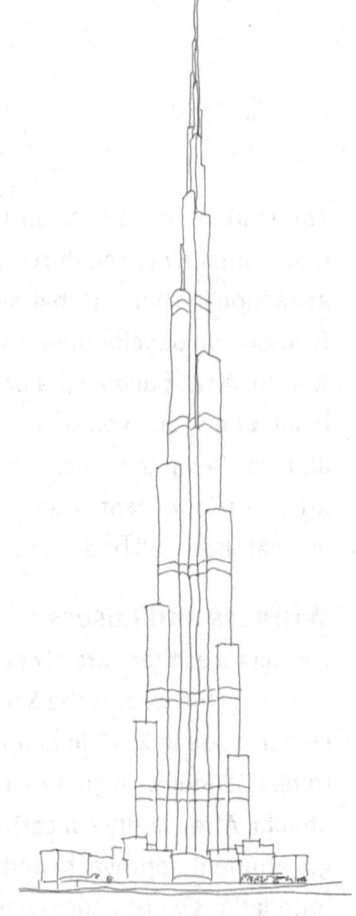

Figure 16: The Burj Khalifa, Dubai.

"The World's tallest building. A living wonder. A stunning work of art. An incomparable feat of engineering. Burj Khalifa is all that. In concept and execution, Burj Khalifa has no peer. More than just the world's tallest building, Burj Khalifa is an unprecedented example of international cooperation, a symbolic beacon of progress, and an emblem of the new, dynamic and prosperous Middle East. It is also tangible proof of Dubai's growing role in a changing world. In fewer

than 30 years, this city has transformed itself from a regional centre to a global one. This success was not based on oil reserves, but on reserves of human talent, ingenuity and initiative. Burj Khalifa embodies that vision."[38]

This statement starts to answer the tall question, the question of *why*. The Burj is the most popular attraction in Dubai. Dubai is running out of oil and has focussed on development to invest their current wealth. A tall building is a bank, you pay money to build it now, and you receive rent, like interest, for its lifetime. Being the tallest building in the world, it attracts a lot of rent, visitors and residents that spend in local shops, all boosting the economy.

Winners and Losers

Like all races there are always far more losers than winners. One loser is the Sky Tower which began construction in 2013 in Changsha China. It was planned to be 838 metres high, ten metres taller than the Burj Khalifa. After safety concerns were raised, the lack of government approval halted the project[39]. The foundations were under construction when work was halted. Rain filled it with water, so now local farmers use it for fish farming.

There are currently 40 projects in the planning stage of development, to be taller than the Burj Khalifa. It is often the role of an urban designer at this stage to conceive a vision that can be defined as 'great'.

Greatness is vital for raising funds and building momentum for the project. Currently, there are eight tallest buildings being planned in the United States, ten in Japan, five in the Arab Emirates and four in China. Other notable locations are Port Sudan, London, Brussels, Cairo, Iraq, Buenos Aires and Brazil.

The Jeddah Tower in Saudi Arabia stalled in 2018, less than a quarter of the way up to the planned 1000 metres in height. The building was originally going to be a mile-high tower, but it was later downgraded to one kilometre[40]. At the time of writing, construction is believed to have recommenced.

There is also the Dubai Creek Tower which began in 2016 and is expected to be complete in 2021. Its height has not been disclosed, but it is to be taller than its neighbour, the Burj Khalifa.

The race for tall began with the Egyptian tombs in glorification of the pharaohs, then the church era, in adoration of the gods. The Eiffel Tower and Washington monument were partially about statehood, yet it was a mixture of private and public funding, of state-supported capitalism. The race continued with the New York buildings which defined this era as a glorification of capitalism. Technology took over with the TV and radio mast period. This era was about maximising viewers, not about creating a landmark and is an era of media and technology.

The Burj Khalifa goes back to the era of capitalism. Please understand, the race for the tallest *building*, rather than *structure*, was always running on the side. The construction of the Griffin Television Tower beating the Empire State Building caused the competition to separate in two, the race for tallest structure and the smaller race for tallest building.

The race for tallest building sees Asia, the Middle East, Europe and North America all compete to be the tallest. The rules about how to define a tall building were redefined to ignore the TV masts. Basically, the definition is a cheat so architectural buildings can win. We have all seen the unusual definition put to landmarks to make them the tallest. Some of my favourites are with, *'the tallest in the southern hemisphere'* or *'tallest in the continent'*, another is Q2 in Queensland, *'the tallest residential building'*.

The Burj Khalifa blows all these factors out the window. It is the tallest of everything. Building, structure, human-made… everything. The contest for tallest building, from the era of capitalism ran a side race for a while but the Burj Khalifa bought the whole competition back into one. It relegated the towers from the era of media, into history.

If the Burj Khalifa is a monument to capitalism, then we must accept that it is also a monument to the classic arguments against capitalism. Workers' rights and the disparity of wealth, all come to the forefront when we look behind the corporate statements. Workers from India, the Philippians, Nepal, Bangladesh, and Pakistan, are all denied citizenship in Dubai. Ninety per cent of the residents are expats. They work twelve-hour shifts while companies withhold pay checks or workers' passports, so they do not quit and return home[41]. Human Rights Watch has singled out the 'kafala' visa sponsorship system as an incredible abuse. This system puts the worker in debt to their employers for flights, contracts and visas. If a worker tries to leave, they face fines or imprisonment. This chapter begins the race with the pyramids where we question if the workers were slaves, and we end in Dubai, asking the same question.

6. Big Things

The race for biggest building was won by the world's largest, the Pentagon in Washington DC - the capital city of the United States of America. This building is so famous, the people inside are referred to by the name of the building. For example, this headline in the New York Times:

"The Pentagon released U.F.O. videos. Don't hold your breath for a breakthrough."[42]

It is impossible for a building to do anything physically, yet it is common for the Department of Defense leaders to be referred to as a building. It is an impressive achievement for a building to be so iconic that it becomes a metonym for the people who use it. The Pentagon is more than just a five-sided shape (how it obtained its name), it has half a million square metres of floor space for 26,000 employees and an 8,770-car parking lot. It also receives 106,000 tourists every year. The architect G. Edwin Bergstrom essentially designed the building as an offset from the five roads around it. It was planned to be next to the Arlington National Cemetery, which caused an eruption of protests due to its large scale near the sacred cemetery. The planners then decided to relocate the building farther east, yet the building design was kept in its original form[43]. Now the Pentagon's shape appears arbitrary and even more iconic. It is the result of an accident of history and not the typical offset from roads. Its status as the biggest in the world is also a result of trying to house the largest military in the world and not from an effort to break any records.

Usually, landmark design is primarily about attracting attention. One of the earliest successful attempts comes from 'Lucy the elephant'. Lucy is twenty metres high; she has windows down her side and telescopes in her eyes to act as an observatory. She was built in 1882 and made of wood and tin. She is shaped as a giant elephant with a four posted arched pagoda on her back. She was created as a public relations stunt by real estate magnate James V. Lafferty who took potential landowners, dressed in top hats and corsets, up inside the stairs through her legs to inside her large belly, then to the pagoda on top to see their new land. (See Figure 17: The internal layout of Lucy the Elephant.)

By 1969 Lucy was looking unwell. She had boarded up windows, a broken trunk with one tusk missing. The local community banded together to form the Save Lucy Committee and successfully raised money for her restoration. As a victory march, she was transported on the back of a truck to her new home in Margate, New Jersey. Taller than a four-storey house, people in flared jeans and miniskirts lined the streets to watch her parade past. Today she looks as young as she did 140 years ago, although Hurricane Sandy blackened the end of her tusk with a bolt of lightning, she is an American National Historic landmark and visited by over 135,000 people a year. She was built as a temporary land sales stunt but outlasted the millennium.

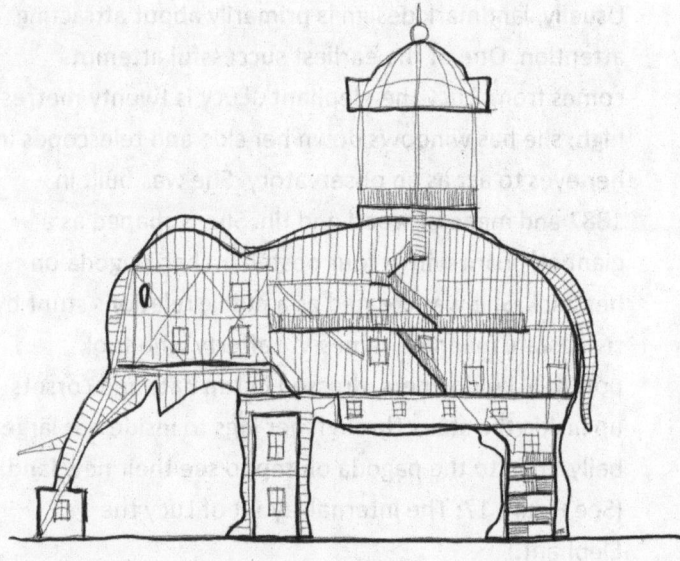

Figure 17: The internal layout of Lucy the Elephant.

Real estate agents have a knack at creating distinctive landmarks throughout history. If we make a comparison of 'big' landmarks with popularity scores and the number of reviews on Tripadvisor.com, then we see the winner is the biggest sign in the world.

The Biggest Sign

The Hollywood Sign, on the Hollywood Hills, is nearly 100 years old and was built by developers SH Woodruff and Tracy E Shoults to promote their new neighbourhood called 'Hollywoodland'. The sign was initially lit up and would blink, "HOLLY", "WOOD" then "LAND", and was only intended to last 18 months. When the great depression hit in the 1930s the caretaker stripped the sign of its copper and sold it for scrap, ending its light display. By 1944, residents who had come to love the sign protested the city's attempt of removal. In 1949 the city removed the word "LAND" from the end of the sign so that it represented the community of Hollywood and not a real estate development. By 1973, the city declared it a 'Los Angeles Cultural and Historical Monument #111'. The sign is now highly respected, with the Department of Homeland Security monitoring the landmark with infrared, motion sensors, razor wire, alarms, and helicopter patrols to keep it safe[44]. (See Figure 18: The Hollywood Sign.)

Figure 18: The Hollywood Sign.

Lucy was one of the first 'big' attractions, and the Hollywood sign is the most successful, both of which pull visitors to their location with no other real purpose beyond tourism.

Big Roadside Attractions

Big things became ubiquitous from the 1950s to the 1980s. Canada has the Big Coin, Big Truck, Big Axe, Fiddle, Salmon and even the Big Ukrainian Lady in the town of Canora. 'Leisa' is dressed in traditional Ukrainian clothing standing seven and a half metres on top of a podium with the slogan, "Welcome to Canora" at its base[45]. She is 75 years old but does not look a day over twenty. She welcomes people passing through the town with her tray of bread, known as *Korovai* in Ukrainian, and with a bowl of salt for the bread to be dipped in. Inscribed at the base of the statue is a plaque commemorating the first group of settlers from Ukraine to the province in 1897. This large, brightly-coloured statue has the multiple functions of celebrating the history and enticing passers-by to stop.

Located one hundred miles from Leisa in Saskatchewan, is the large Indian Head statue. It is a giant disembodied head on a stone column situated at a tourist information point. Initially, this seems racially awkward as a landmark, but the statue is in honour of the town, which is called Indian Head. Dan L. noted the following on TripAdvisor,

"This statue was built in 1985, the total height is 18 feet, head height is 10 feet, base is 8 feet. It weighs 3,500 pounds and is constructed of metal pipe, metal mesh and [with] three coats of cement. Coloration was applied by incorporating cement pigments into the final cement coat. The statue was designed by Don Foulds from Saskatoon, SK at a cost of $12,750 and transported to Indian Head. The statue has appeared in numerous television commercials and is located in the southwest corner of the town of Indian Head on the north side of Highway #1."[46]

It would seem the designer simply took the name of the town literally and designed a sculpture depicting precisely - an American indigenous person's head. Yet, looking deeper into the history of how the town got its name, I initially thought 'head' referred to a landscape feature, the true meaning is revealed on the town's website,

"Many First Nations people were stricken by diseases like smallpox, which were introduced by fur traders who travelled through this area. Local First Nations people used the hills south of the current town site as their burial grounds, but many bodies were not buried at all, so great was the fear of contracting the disease. Over the years the First Nations people came to call the burial ground the Many Skeletons Hills or Many Skulls Hills. The new settlers who came to the area referred to them as the Indian Head Hills."[47]

As a roadside attraction, the Big Indian Head has a dark and more profound meaning than the sculpture offers at first glance. The design of the brightly-coloured, alive-looking head does not depict this history. I doubt if the truth were well known, this roadside attraction would lose its function of enticing visitors to stop.

Australia has 159 'big things'[48]. It is home to the famous Big Pineapple, Big Banana, Big Chook, Lobster, Merino (sheep) and the Big Potato in the town of Robertson. This landmark could easily be missed as it looks like a rounded one and a half storey boulder. I guess it is hard to depict a potato beyond a big brown lump. Australia is a large country with a sparse population so 'big' roadside attractions are constructed to entice tourists off the highway into the towns to stop and, more importantly, spend. An example of this is in the more arid regions of the country.

A major drought in the Australian state of Victoria from 1877 to 1884 prompted the then Prime Minister of Australia, Alfred Deakin, to begin irrigation of the desert around the intersection of three state borders. Plans for the settlement in this new region were to rival the large metropolises of California, with foreign experts shipped over to help with the scheme. The irrigation of this outback desert area was a success, and now the region is famous for its fresh fruit. The vision to have millions of people living here was less successful, with Mildura never getting close to the size of Los Angeles or San Diego even though the city plans are prepared for this future population.

If you are driving along the National Highway from Mildura to South Australia's capital, Adelaide, just outside of the town of Renmark you are met with a new bypass road turning off to the right. It is the fastest way to Adelaide. Yet, if you drive straight, via the longer route, you will go through the famous fruit town of Berri. If you were perhaps on a family trip with kids in the back seat, arguing, what decision would you make? Like many people, you would probably take the faster bypass. Well, guess what you just missed? Just four hundred metres down the road is the landmark of the World's Biggest Orange. A fifteen-metre-high ball of orange metal standing in the scorching sun. It sits in the middle of a field with a few sheds and a train carriage. It has a green leaf painted on its top with a green circular pipe that I assume is meant to be a stem. A balcony near the top allows visitors who climb its stairs to look out across the landscape. The landmark was from the 1980s when Australians explored their country by caravan. The Big Orange was then the destination of choice.

University of South Australia lecturer Dr Ben Stubbs said to ABC News,

"When there weren't the bypasses and freeways, you would stop off, and it would be part of your trip to go and look at the Big Orange, the Big Merino, the Big Pineapple."[49]

You were right to take the bypass. The Big Orange is closed. A broken sign lays propped against the locked gate stating this fact, and you saved your children from disappointment. The orange trees have been removed due to a further drought, and the owner went into liquidation. Yet a 'big' attraction still functions as an *attraction*, closed or not.

Late at night, when all is dark, visitors (perhaps drunk), will climb the fence, sneak in, probably laughing and talking way too loudly, will attempt to climb the landmark. The current owner's night job is to get up from his couch and frighten the visitors away, night after night.

As a further insult, there is an online petition trying to turn the Orange into a strip club. The change.org petition reads-

"For too long the Riverland's biggest tourist attraction, The Big Orange has sat wasting away. Well stick this in your pipe and smoke it, folks! The big orange strip club, volunteer strippers. Fully licensed. Kids room. Discounts for pensioners."[50]

Judging by the lack of activity on the petition, the Orange will have to wait for another investment proposal.

Two of the most successful 'big' roadside attractions in Australia are the Big Pineapple and the Big Banana. Both are initially Agri-tourism (agricultural-tourism) attractions, on major highways between two tourism regions. The Pineapple is on the Sunshine Coast, north of Brisbane on the drive up the coast, and the Banana located between Sydney and Brisbane. Both have kept their location on the highway and have not been affected by a bypass. They are both a product of their time. The Banana was built in 1964 and the Pineapple in 1971, and now on the heritage register. They both have managed to survive. The long concrete Banana (you walk in one end, learn about banana plantations, and exit the other end) now has a waterpark, minigolf, indoor ice skating, a theatre, and many food outlets. The Pineapple has struggled, but it has a zoo now, a zipline course, a train, and hosts a music festival. They have become more than a shaped piece of concrete and fibreglass, with many adults today remembering their childhood trips up the coast, wanting their children to experience the same thing. Many adults believe these landmarks have been reduced in size with a segment of conspiracy theorists believing the Banana was rebuilt to be smaller. The owners insist it was never rebuilt, it was just moved closer to the highway, and they point out that many adults have grown up since their first visit making themselves bigger, not the landmark smaller.

One metre taller than the Queensland Big Pineapple is the South African Big Pineapple at Bathurst. Constructed in the 1990s, it is a museum to the agricultural history of the region. It is a copy of the Queensland Pineapple with an observation deck around the sprouting green leaf roof ornamentation.

New Zealand does not escape the race for big attractions. They are home to the Trout, Carrot, Salmon, Sand-fly and of course the Big Kiwi Fruit. Kiwi 360 is a slice of Kiwi Fruit with a lookout at the top. The reason for a cut, and not a whole fruit, is an attempt to avoid the Big Potato's appearance of just looking like a big rock, as kiwis look just as round and simple in colour. The slice shows the seeds with the core and is unmistakeably a kiwifruit.

Europe, with its sophisticated tourist attractions in the form of historic landmarks, also brings us the Woinic

Boar. A series of steel sheets welded over a frame in the shape of a pig. It has a slight comic book appearance and watches over Autoroute A34 in France. Germany also manages to get the biggest Coffee Pot in, although it is only around one and a half storeys in height, it still prompts people passing through the town of Selb to stop off for a photo and a coffee.

The real winner of the country with the most 'biggest' things is, of course, the United States of America. In analysing these, I found the list getting out of hand and ended with recording only 235 of them. Pecans are prevalent, so are pencils. There is the largest ball of twine wars, documented in the podcast 99 Percent Invisible[51], where the two towns of Darwin and Cawker City started competing for the largest ball of twine in the world. Over time, each attempted to make theirs larger. The situation was resolved by a definition, with Darwin receiving the title of *Largest Ball of Twine in the world made by one man*, and the whole town of Cawker City all having a role in producing the *Largest Ball of Twine* in total size. As a side note, twine is used in farming and is often discarded after use, hence the accumulation of 5,000 pounds (2,267 kilograms) at 8 feet high (2.4 metres) for the Cawker City record.

There is the Largest Squirting Clam in Long Beach, Washington. In 2002 when the annual Clam Festival was mothballed, the clam disappeared. It returned with the revival of the festival in 2014, and standing at 1.5 metres high with a shell made of driftwood it shoots water a few metres into the air. I wonder if the reason for it 'spitting' could be related to the fact a giant pan is just next to it, threatening to cook it. The clam spits for free on the hour or spits on demand for a quarter[52]. This is one of the most bizarre landmarks I have researched.

The most impressive 'big' thing would have to be Ohio's Big Basket Building. Opened in 1997, it is a large version of the Longaberger's shopping basket. The company that owned the building, and manufacturer of the baskets, created this giant box-like shopping basket as their headquarters. It is around 7 to 8 storeys high with windows located on the inward weave of the basket's wicker appearance, on every second row. Two giant handles are atop the building stretching a few more storeys above its roof. The whole building is a yellowish orange. The inside has a dignified mock Victorian-styled courtyard with windowed elevators and a glass atrium roof. The company ceased operation in 2019, and on October the 20th, over 600 people came for a tour of the big basket, fearing the building was to be demolished. The following day it was announced the basket would reopen as a luxury hotel[53].

The Big Statue Race
Big structures are not limited to roadside attractions, with large statues taking over as the most dominant

big attraction in recent times. Large statues come in two forms, either being of gods or people, yet the most famous figure is of both.

The Sphinx of Giza dates from around 2532 BCE and is a half-lion, half-human hybrid. Egyptologists believe its face is that of pharaoh Khafre who is considered a god to the ancient Egyptians. The Sphinx depicts an animal, human and god, all combined into one. This is unique in the list of large statues.

The most famous statue, and the highest-ranked in the greatest landmarks list, is the Statue of Liberty in New York City, USA. The artist, Frederic Bartholdi named it "Liberty Enlightening the World", with the name 'Statue of Liberty' purely a nickname. It was designed and built in France as a gift to the United States to commemorate their Declaration of Independence in 1886. It was meant to inspire the French to overthrow their ruler, Napoleon III. The cost of the statue was taken up by a mixture of French and American benefactors with 80% of the US$102,000 being raised from sums of less than one dollar from average people inspired by the project. Early funding difficulties nearly led the statue to be built in Boston or Philadelphia when groups offered to pay the full cost of the construction in return for its relocation. The skeleton of the figure was built of iron pylon and steel that allows the copper skin to move independently during strong winds[54].

Her greatness is not only due to its remarkable engineering feat, or physical size and location in the centre of New York Harbor, but due to how much she is loved. Throughout history, from her crowdfunding origin to a centrepiece for fireworks and celebrations today, she has always been adored. Nothing represents the core values of the United States of America more through her representation of 'liberty' and 'freedom'. She is a UNESCO Heritage protected site, attributed with the following statement,

The symbolic value of the Statue of Liberty lies in two basic factors. It was presented by France with the intention of affirming the historical alliance between the two nations. It was financed by international subscription in recognition of the establishment of the principles of freedom and democracy by the United States of America's Declaration of Independence, which the Statue holds in her left hand. The Statue also soon became and has endured as a symbol of the migration of people from many countries into the United States in the late 19th and the early 20th centuries. She endures as a highly potent symbol – inspiring contemplation, debate, and protest – of ideals such as liberty, peace, human rights, the abolition of slavery, democracy, and opportunity[55].

When it comes to statue height, *Lady Liberty* ranks as far down as 49th tallest in the world. Above her are fifteen large Buddha statues and sixteen large statues of the eastern god Guanyin, amongst others. The largest statue in the world at present is the 'Statue of Unity' depicting Sardar Vallabhbhai Patel in India.

The Statue of Unity passed the Statue of Liberty in average daily visitors of 15,000 per day just a year after it opened in 2018. This astounding magnet to tourists stands at 182 metres (597 feet) high. It is located in the Shoolpaneshwar Wildlife Sanctuary on the northern bank of the Narmada River; seven hours drive north of Mumbai. Its representation of India's first Home Minister, Sadar Patel is realistic in style, wearing traditional clothing, both arms lowered to his side and depicted in his later years. His big toe is taller than a person. His ear is larger than a house. The construction is remarkable, as it shows Sadar in a dhoti and his feet in sandals requiring the statue to be thinner on the bottom. This form trades off stability for design, which all other tall statues have been unable to achieve. (See Figure 19.)

Figure 19: Height comparison. From left to right- The Statue of Unity (182m), Spring Temple Buddha, China (128m), Ushiku

Daibutsu, Japan (120m), Statue of Liberty, New York (93m), The motherland calls, Russia (85m), Christ the Redeemer, Brazil (39.6m).

As with all great landmarks, the attention they attract is not always positive. In 2020, due to the COVID19 financial crisis, the attraction was offered up for sale for around five million dollars.

The ad read, *"Emergency! Selling Statue of Unity because of urgent money required for Hospitals and healthcare equipment."*[56]

Of course, it turned out to be a scam, with the seller placing the ad to defame the government and mislead people. *"Such an advertisement hurts the sentiments of several crore people who idolise Sardar Patel."*[57] said the administrator of the landmark.

Another tall statue, standing at 71 metres high is the Leshan Giant Buddha. Ranked as the 20th tallest in the world, it was built between 713 to 803AD. It is carved into the red stone bank of the Dadu River south of Chengdu, in central China. Its toes are also the size of a person, although the god is seated therefore does not reach the Statue of Unity's height due to the height limitation of the cliff face into which it is carved. Visitors arrive on the top side of the rock face and walk down a steep set of stairs near the statue's right hand to its feet only one storey above the raging river. The jungle has reclaimed parts of the figure, with moss on its shoulders and around its legs.

Its UNESCO World Heritage statement lists it as:

"Buddhism was introduced into China in the 1st century CE via the Silk Road from India to Mount Emei, and it was on Mount Emei that the first Buddhist temple in China was built."[58]

After the greatest and biggest statues, the Mansudae Art Studio of the secretive North Korea would have to win the race for the most prolific producers of giant statues. The studio has around 4,000 people with 800 artists, in a 12-hectare sized studio. It was founded in 1959, six years after the Korean War. The studio is divided into 13 creative groups, seven manufacturing plants and more than 50 supply departments[59]. The studio produces everything from oil paintings to embroideries, yet what is most impressive are its large bronze statues.

A fascinating example of their work is of two giant statues next to each other of the leaders Kim Il-sung and Kim Jong-il. They stand at around six storeys with both looking to the horizon smiling. Kim Il-sung has his arm up with a hand open as if pointing to something in the distance. The statues are very realistic. They have creases in their trousers, buttons on their coats and hollows in their cuffs. They are made of polished copper, not the green copper of the Statue of Liberty which oxidised after a couple of years of weathering. The studio has produced other propaganda-inspired large groups of statues. One-piece shows Kim Jong-il, hand over a girl's shoulder looking out to the horizon, a young couple on his left holds a basket of flowers looking at him in admiration with three people on his right and an old movie camera between them. One individual has a notebook as if recording his words. The seven statues are again very realistic, in copper and highly detailed.

The studio has also produced a lot of work outside of North Korea as well. A gigantic copper statue known as the African Renaissance Monument was fabricated by the studio to commemorate the 50th anniversary of Senegal's independence from France. It stands at 52 metres high with a shirtless man holding a baby hoisted on his shoulder with one hand pointing to the distance and his other hand around the curve of a woman's back as if lifting them all to the sky. (See Figure 20.) This sculpture is more stylised than the others, as it is based on a design from Senegalese architect Pierre Goudiaby. At its unveiling, protesters gathered and criticised the statue as being un-Islamic and a waste of money. The AFP news reported,

"The demonstration was called to protest, 'all the failures of Wade's regime, the least of which is this horrible statue'. Deputy opposition leader Ndeye Fatou Toure said the statue was an 'economic monster and a financial scandal in the context of the current [economic] crisis'."[60]

It was revealed later that the country was unable to pay the $27 million in cash, so a deal was made of state-owned land as payment[61].

Figure 20: The African Renaissance Monument.

Botswana also has Mansudae Art Studio statues. Three, in fact. Known as the 'Three Dikgosi Monument', it depicts the three tribal chiefs Khama III of the Bangwato, Sebele I of the Bakwena, and Bathoen I of the Bangwaketse. These three statues stand with each other at the height of two storeys. They have tremendous detail, bronze and realistic, all looking towards various parts of the horizon. The statues are the largest tourist attraction in the capital of Gaborone.

The studio has also produced a statue in the form of a memorial to Ethiopian and Cuban soldiers involved in the Ogaden War known as the Tiglachin Monument, in Ethiopia. In Benin, the studio built a statue memorializing the 11th king of Dahomey, Béhanzin. He is known for leading the indigenous resistance efforts against French colonisation in the 1890s. In Europe, the studio was commissioned to restore Frankfurt's Fairy Tale Fountain, an art nouveau sculpture from 1910 that was melted down for its metal during World War II. The studio was chosen for its early 1900s-style and was tasked to recreate the fountain based on old photographs[62].

Of the top 100 tallest statues in the world, one third were built since 2010 and the next third built since the millennium. The big statue race for tall is a race that is heating up right now. First China, Japan and then India are running this race with statues appearing at three to four a year. This race is a tourism race, a race for visitors. The tourism industry refers to these attractions as flagships – an iconic attraction that functions only to bring tourists to a destination. Statues epitomise flagship attractions as they have little use other than tourism. Buddha and Guanyin statues, also their Mary and Jesus counterparts, are a symbol to be worshipped but also function as flagship attractions.

Big statues and big roadside attractions make for excellent landmarks and can be successful at attracting interest depending on their size. They do not win the race for the greatest landmarks, yet they do gain very high positions on the list.

The most successful big things are a mix of size and meaning. The larger, the better but also, the deeper its meaning, the more successful it will be. The most successful large landmark is the Statue of Liberty with remarkable associations of liberty and freedom. Whereas the Big Orange, although very large, has an uninteresting meaning, and its greatness and number of visitors suffer for that.

7. The Race for Meaning

"For the meaning of life differs from man to man, from day to day and from hour to hour. What matters, therefore, is not the meaning of life in general but rather the specific meaning of a person's life at a given moment." Viktor E. Frankl.

The meaning behind a landmark is one of the most critical measures of greatness. Its height and its popularity attract attention, but its meaning is what encourages people to stay and enjoy it. The stories visitors learn, and the experiences they have are what they tell friends at home. Sadly today, with social media being so dominant, tourists do not stop and understand the meaning of landmark. They simply take a photo, upload it to Instagram and then travel to the next location. A significant tourist attraction in the state of Victoria, Australia is the journey along the Great Ocean Road. The foremost landmark on this tourist trail is the Twelve Apostles, a series of stone pillars out in the ocean formed by the waves eating away at the coastline. Farmland drops away to a cliff and these pillars in the ocean stand where the land once stood hundreds of years ago. (See Figure 21.)

Figure 21: The Twelve Apostles.

Along this coast is the Bay of Martyrs, renamed from Massacre Bay as it was considered more palatable to tourists. Its name comes from a historical event when Europeans, to save bullets, ran all the Karrae-Wurrong Aboriginal men off the cliff and then went back and murdered the women and children in a horrific act of genocide. A filtered Instagram photo of rocks will not communicate this.

All is not lost though. If designers and tourism experts conveyed these stories better, an Instagram photo could communicate a lot more. In assessing the Great Ocean Road, I had the idea of placing a series of statues along the trail depicting moments from history. It would be a contentious series of landmarks, especially the story of Massacre Bay, but it would have an impact and can communicate more than just a sign.

Interpreting the meaning of a location is in the realm of tourism studies and the humanities. The days of simply putting up a sign and writing out the story of a site are not good enough anymore. Tour guides are one of the best ways of explaining stories, but the bar needs to be lifted to capture the fast-paced, image-focused, tourism consumer of today. Tourists want to gain an understanding and move on quickly. The advancements in the field of tourism interpretation are at the forefront of communication. It is becoming so sophisticated that other fields are learning from it. Do you remember when we used to go into a retail shop and buy a simple cup of coffee and move on? The coffee shop industry has learnt from tourism by creating a *coffee experience,* and so have breweries and the wine industry. You do not just buy a coffee, bottle of wine or a beer; we now get tours, we have explanations of the coffee beans and the social responsibility behind the sourcing of the beans. We have winery tours and learn about how wine is made, and at breweries, we are taught about hops and barley and the fermentation process. I predict in twenty years most retail shops will be about the experience, to compete with online stores. Apple® does this already with their stores, and Starbucks® has a coffee display like what you would see in a history museum. In the future we will learn about how clothing is made (and the lack of exploitation), experience kneading of the dough at bakeries, or sample the taste of various breakfast cereals at a Kellogg's® store.

Therefore, all is not lost in the race for meaning, but landmarks and tourism destinations need to pick up the pace to communicate some of the most amazing, horrific and beautiful stories our world has to offer so that they can be snapped on a smartphone.

Initially, in researching the world's greatest landmarks and measuring the quantity of meaning associated with a landmark, I thought we only needed to measure its age. The older a landmark, the more history laid stories upon it. The results were significantly flawed. I found in my city, a beach pavilion of considerable age compared to the Houses of Parliament or the Exhibition Centre where the first national government was formed. Natural features also suffer this fate. For example, a boulder near a landmark would be far older than the landmark next to it.

Furthermore, the meaning (or cultural value) of a landmark, whether it is an Indian Head, a Big Orange or the Statue of Liberty, is often more important than the built form or look of the object. For example, if the Sagrada Familia, Gaudi's famous cathedral were built for devil worship, its fame would be seriously reduced. It seemed an impossible task to measure the meaning of a landmark until I discovered the UNESCO World Heritage evaluations.

UNESCO

The United Nations Educational, Scientific and Cultural Organization was formed in 1946 and based in Paris. There are 193 member countries and 11 associate members. UNESCO World Heritage Sites are locations nominated by a government as locations of cultural or natural importance and placed on a Tentative List. The International Council on Monuments and Sites and the International Union for Conservation of Nature, then evaluate the sites and make recommendations to the World Heritage Committee. The areas are evaluated under ten criteria. To achieve just one condition achieves the status of a UNESCO World Heritage Site. Registration has the impact of raising the site's international prestige and attracts conservation efforts and tourists, yet in some cases, it can put the area at risk of over-tourism. There is an Aboriginal Australian Stonehenge in the State of Victoria which predates the English landmark by thousands of years. The site is incredibly sensitive and any attempt at prescribing the location as a UNESCO World Heritage site has been shut down for its protection. Alternatively, in 2016, the Australian government successfully managed to stop UNESCO from reporting the Great Barrier Reef as a site 'at risk' by getting it removed from the report, 'World Heritage and Tourism in a Changing Climate'. The government felt the label would impact tourism revenue, as people would believe it is destroyed[63].

UNESCO status acts as a driver of international attention that benefits the wider community. When I was working in India on the construction of a new town to house workers of a steel mill, the decision was made to capitalise on the world heritage status of the local Hampi site. Our concept was to create a corridor park with stone pavilions and activity spaces that reflected the construction famous in the heritage site. This creates a connection to the Hampi ruins and boosts the concept for *placemaking* purposes. (*Placemaking* is an urban design process used to create uniqueness and an individual identity for a location, to prevent cookie-cutter towns from all being the same.)

The criteria to achieve UNESCO World Heritage status is divided into ten categories. The first six are attributed to cultural merit and the second four are to natural qualities. When these criteria are combined with the original bucket list of great landmarks, it adds an additional layer of information to help us understand what aspects are important in creating a great landmark in relation to their meaning.

Masterpieces
Criterion (i) is- *"A masterpiece of human creative genius"*[64]

UNESCO lists the Taj Mahal as *"the jewel of Muslim art in India and one of the universally admired masterpieces of the world's heritage"*[65].

It meets the first criterion as a masterpiece of human creative genius but does not achieve any of the other criteria. The landmark stands at the height of 73 metres on the southern bank of the Yamuna river, in Agra, India. This pristinely white mausoleum stands on a square stone plinth with four minarets in each corner and a rectangular building in the centre. The building has four smaller domes in each corner and one gigantic dome at its centre rising seventy-three metres. Gardens surround the landmark, measuring one kilometre by three hundred metres. The gardens accentuate the solitary height of the structure. (See Figure 22.) An area of 10,400 square kilometres around the complex is defined to protect the landmark from pollution. UNESCO notes as part of its heritage status,

The Supreme Court of India, in December 1996, delivered a ruling banning use of coal/coke in industries located in the Taj Trapezium Zone (TTZ) and switching over to natural gas or relocating them outside the TTZ. The TTZ comprises of 40 protected monuments including three World Heritage Sites - Taj Mahal, Agra Fort and Fatehpur Sikri.[65]

News reports in 2018 point to the issues the Taj is experiencing which include the white marble turning yellow and green due to poor air quality, the garbage piling up on its riverside bank and, *"Tiny insects from the drying Yamuna River, into which the city pours its sewage, crawl into the Taj Mahal, their excrement further staining the marble..."*[66]

Its creative genius distinguishes the landmark due to, *"Its recognised architectonic beauty has a rhythmic combination of solids and voids, concave and convex and light shadow; such as arches and domes further increases the aesthetic aspect. The colour combination of lush green scape reddish pathway and blue sky over it showcases the monument in ever changing tints and moods. The relief work in marble and inlay with precious and semi-precious stones make it a monument apart."*[65]

Figure 22: The Taj Mahal, India.

Other landmarks that achieve only this first criterion are the Sydney Opera House and Sydney Harbour Bridge in Australia, and the Temple of Preah Vihear in

Cambodia along with many other landmarks of importance that meet this criterion and others in the UNESCO list.

Human Cultural Interchange

Criterion (ii)- *"Exhibits an important interchange of human values, over a span of time or within a cultural area of the world, on developments in architecture, technology, monumental arts, town-planning or landscape design"*[64]

Masjed-e Jāmé in Iran and the Missions of San Antonio, Texas, in the United States of America, are the only landmarks listed that achieve only this category (ii). There are five missions in San Antonio with the complexes built over a 12.4 kilometre stretch of the San Antonio Basin. Built during the 18th century, they were a Spanish attempt to colonise, evangelise and defend the northern frontier of New Spain. The Missions represent the merging of Spanish and Indigenous cultures with the Mission of Valero, also known as the Alamo, being a famous example.

Authenticity is a critical component to UNESCO classification with these churches, *"...in the 19th century, structures were added to the complexes and these were even extended or modernized in the 20th century. However, the stratigraphy of the different consecutive additions is clearly legible in most sites and early physical remains can be easily identified."*[67]

Another notable landmark which meets criterion (ii), amongst other measures, is the Mogao Caves in Gansu Province, China. This landmark is located in the country's north-west desert. If travelling by tour bus, you will cross a broad, light-coloured, dusty desert to a river that runs along the edge of a mountain range. For thousands of years, the river has scooped out soil from the base of these mountains creating a cliff escarpment from midway down its slope to its base. This cliff face is around two kilometres long and has 492 caves carved in it. There are 45,000 square metres of murals and 2,000 painted sculptures ranging from the 4th to the 14th centuries. It is unusual for a cave to be a landmark due to its hidden nature and its inability to help in indicating direction. Yet the main feature of this cliff face is a nine-storey temple (cave 96), carved into the rock and protruding forward. It has a series of pagoda-type roof forms painted in red, and makes an impact as a landmark. (See Figure 23: Cave 96, Mago Caves.)

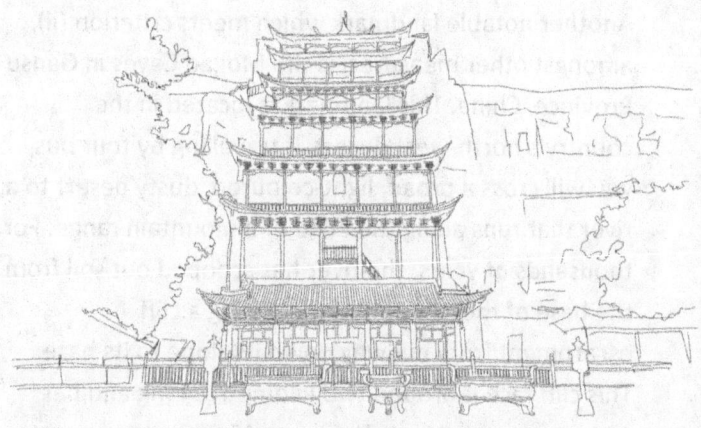

Figure 23: Cave 96, Mago Caves.

The discovery of the Dunhuang library cave in 1990, *"together with the tens of thousands of manuscripts and relics, [this] has been acclaimed as the world's greatest discovery of ancient Oriental culture. This significant heritage provides invaluable reference for studying the complex history of ancient China and Central Asia."*[68]

The caves have a large Buddha statue carved into its face and hundreds of smaller temples and houses. Its note for criteria (ii) is attributed to the cultural exchange the site achieved due to its location on the Silk Road. The note is as follows,

"For 1,000 years, from the period of the Northern Wei Dynasty (386-534) to the Mongol-led Yuan Dynasty (1276-1386), the caves of Mogao played a decisive role in artistic exchanges between China, Central Asia and India."[68]

A Cultural Tradition

Criteria (iii) is, *"To bear a unique or at least exceptional testimony to a cultural tradition or to a civilization which is living or which has disappeared"*[64]

The Al Qal'a of Beni Hammad site lies one hundred kilometres south of the Mediterranean coastline, on the southern side of a mountain range that marks the flourishing areas of Algeria with the deserts of North Africa. Its appointment to the UNESCO World Heritage list follows its acceptance to criteria (iii) by bearing exceptional testimony to the Hammadid civilisation now disappeared. Its UNESCO Heritage statement tells of its history,

"Founded in 1007 as a military stronghold, it was elevated to the level of metropolis. It has influenced the development of Arab architecture as well as other civilizing influences, including the Maghreb, Andalusia and Sicily. The archaeological and monumental vestiges of the Qal'a of Beni Hammad, among which are included the Great mosque and its minaret as well as a series of palaces, constitute the principal resources that testify to the wealth and influence of this Hammadid civilization."[69]

Originally, the fort was a walled town. The wall stretched up a mountain slope, around a cluster of buildings and down to the valley below. Today the site looks like a series of ruins with many of the features only evident by their foundations. A square tower still survives, the only real landmark feature on what appears to be a hillside on a rocky desert. Its physical form is unremarkable, but its meaning and importance to human history, and as a record of a lost civilisation are incredibly important.

The Gaocheng Astronomical Observatory achieves criterion (iii), among others, due to its cultural connection to the astronomical idea of being at the centre of heaven and earth. The observatory was built during the Yuan Dynasty (1279-1368) in China and is a device for measuring the length of the sun's shadow at noon and tracing its variations throughout the year. The United Nations Portal to Heritage explains,

"The platform is 9.45m high and its sides are over 16m long at the base and over 8m long at the top. On the northern part of the platform stand two rooms separated by an opening... A horizontal rod connects the two rooms through their facing windows, and directly below this a groove with vertical sides runs down the centre of the north side of the platform. The scale, which is called the sky-measuring scale, was built using 36 stone blocks... Two parallel troughs run along the top of the scale; they are linked at the ends and would have held water to form a level surface... On either side of the scale at its north end are two reconstructed astronomical instruments that were originally invented by Guo Shoujing. On the eastern side is the zheng fang an, or 'square meter', while to

the west is the yang yi, a type of sundial using a spherical surface."[70]

This tall landmark tower was built as a purely functional design with its dimensions based on sun angles rather than an aesthetic appreciation. It is a testament to science and the cultural importance of astronomy during this period. (See Figure 24.)

Figure 24: The Gaocheng Astronomical Observatory.

A Significant Stage of Human History

Criterion (iv) is, *"To be an outstanding example of a type of building, architectural, technological ensemble* *or landscape which illustrates a significant stage in human history."*

The Ōta River flows down from the mountains in Japan to a flat estuary on the edge of a bay. The upstream river cuts deep into the land as gravity pulls it over falls and down rapids. When it arrives at the estuary, the river is subdued and at its lowest point. The land is flat and so close to sea level, it meanders in all directions and forks in two, multiple times. It is on the banks of the river at one of these forks, where this landmark is sited. The Product Exhibition Hall building, initially designed by the Czech architect Jan Letzel, was built in April 1915 and was the centre of a large business district. Arts and educational exhibitions were conducted under its five-storey high, domed roof.

At 8:15 am, on 6 August 1945, the United States Army Air Force dropped the first atomic bomb to be used in war from a B-29 bomber. It exploded before it hit the ground to cause maximum impact releasing a mushroom-shaped cloud over the City of Hiroshima, killing 70,000 people instantly. 70,000 more suffered fatal injuries from the radiation. The Product Exhibition Hall was at the epicentre of the blast. The metal supports for the dome managed to survive along with its supporting cylindrical walls. The four-storey high façade facing the river, also survived, as did all the ground floor walls. No part of the roof except the dome supports survived the blast. It is now known as the Hiroshima Peace Memorial, or more casually, as the Atomic Bomb Dome. It meets only criterion (iv) for the following reason,

"The Hiroshima Peace Memorial (Genbaku Dome) is a stark and powerful symbol of the achievement of world peace for more than half a century following the unleashing of the most destructive force ever created by humankind."[71]

The memorial captures, like a camera, the significant moment in history which changed the world.

The UNESCO analysis goes further,

"The Hiroshima Peace Memorial (Genbaku Dome) stands in its original location and its form, design, materials, substance, and setting are all completely authentic. It also maintains its functional and spiritual authenticity as a place for prayer for world peace and the ultimate elimination of all nuclear weapons."[71]

Human and Environmental Interaction

Criterion (v)- *"To be an outstanding example of a traditional human settlement, land-use, or sea-use which is representative of a culture, or human interaction with the environment especially when it has become vulnerable under the impact of irreversible change."[64]*

There are few landmarks to meet only this criterion due to its aim at representing broad areas of settlement. The Old Town of Ghadamès, Libya, is an example of this, and in the past, I have researched its urban form to determine a traditional Libyan-style for the designs of new Libyan towns.

The greatest landmark that meets this criterion along with other measures is the Christ the Redeemer statue on top of Mount Corcovado in Rio De Janeiro, Brazil.

The UNESCO statement for this criterion focusses less on the landmark statue and more on the environment around it and the mountain. It is registered as follows,

"The development of the city of Rio de Janeiro has been shaped by a creative fusion between nature and culture. This interchange is not the result of persistent traditional processes but rather reflects an interchange based on scientific, environmental and design ideas that led to innovative landscape creations on a major scale in the heart of the city during little more than a century. These processes have created an urban landscape perceived to be of great beauty by many writers and travellers and one that has shaped the culture of the city."[72]

The location is over 7,000 hectares with another 8,600-hectare buffer. It is a lush, green, natural mountain range surrounded by a city. It has sheer rock cliffs which surround the statue, lifting it three-quarters of a kilometre above the famous Copacabana and Ipanema beaches below. Sugarloaf Mountain is also included in this classification. It is the renowned cone-shaped mountain that shears down to the water's edge. The origins of its name are contested between the Tamoios Indian words of 'Pau-nh-açuquã' for the mountain and the same Portuguese words of 'Pão de Açúcar', meaning *sugar loaf*, being one explanation. A result of a confusion of language.

Both the mountain and the statue are great landmarks located six kilometres from each other and rising to an immense height, looking over the top of Rio de Janeiro to each other. (See Figure 25.)

Figure 25: Christ the Redeemer statue with Sugar Loaf Mountain in the background.

Significant Events and Achievements

Criterion (vi) *"To be directly or tangibly associated with events, living traditions, with ideas, with beliefs or with artistic and literary works of outstanding universal significance."*[64]

The UNESCO Committee prefers this criterion to be used in conjunction with other criteria. Yet there are five landmarks from meta bucket list which meet only this criterion. They are the Entrance Gate at Auschwitz, the Fort d'Estrées in Senegal, the Rila Monastery in Bulgaria, L'Anse aux Meadows in Canada and the Stari Most Bridge in Bosnia and Herzegovina.

The Auschwitz Entrance Gate is not architecturally significant and may not be considered a landmark, as its size is no bigger than a truck and it has more prominent buildings around it. The metal letters over the gate say ominously in German "arbeit macht frei", 'work sets you free'. The Nazis used this site for the extermination of 960,000 Jewish people (865,000 of whom were gassed on arrival), 74,000 non-Jewish Polish, 21,000 Roma (gypsies), 15,000 Soviet prisoners of war and 15,000 other Europeans. The landmark represents a historical atrocity and stands as a reminder of this bleak history.

The Stari Most Bridge is also a symbol of human malice. Built in the 16th century in the city of Mostar, the bridge crosses the Neretva River connecting each half of the city. The history channel reported back in 1993,

"Over 400 years after its completion, the bridge was destroyed during the conflict that engulfed Bosnia. Under the command of Slobodan Praljak, the Croat militia shelled the bridge as part of its effort to drive

Muslim Bosnians from the predominantly Catholic Croat western half of the city. The eastern half of Mostar, complete with stone mosques and minarets, is home to the majority of the city's Muslim population."[73]

After the war, the bridge was reconstructed and became a symbol of reconciliation. The bridge was rebuilt with local materials and original construction techniques. Hungarian army divers recovered stones of the original bridge from the river below, although most were too damaged to use. The bridge was completed in 2004.

Natural Beauty

Criterion (vii), *"To contain superlative natural phenomena or areas of exceptional natural beauty and aesthetic importance."*

There are only two landmarks on the meta bucket list that fit only this criterion, and they are both mountains.

Mount Kilimanjaro in Tanzania is only 350 kilometres south of the Equator, in the tropics, yet this mountain is covered in snow and glaciers.

A trek to the peak of this iconic landmark takes about nine days due to the extinct volcano's solitary position in the landscape. This also means a trekker can approach from any side. There are seven routes to the summit with the Marangu (Coca Cola) and Machame

(Whiskey) routes, both having considerable hiking traffic[74].

When arriving at Mount Kilimanjaro National Park, the rangers meet trekkers at the gate and measure the porter's bags to ensure no bag is over 20 kilos. This law is strictly adhered to, as it prevents porters from being injured. The hike begins in the jungle on a dirt track winding through thick ferny hills and gullies, complete with birds and monkeys. When the climb begins, the altitude becomes immediately apparent as the thinner air requires more breaths to supply oxygen to the body. The atmosphere changes are why a longer nine-day trek is advisable to help the body adjust to the changes in height. At 3,000 metres above sea level, the trekker emerges from the jungle into a zone of low-lying shrubs and grasses. It is the last time where a full meal can be enjoyed due to the altitude sickness difficulties later in the hike.

The porters in the morning sing songs to get ready and infuse excitement for the day's hike. For a group of three to four trekkers, three times as many porters are needed. The next destination is the Moorlands. This area is a rocky flat saddle area between Mawenzi Peak and the central peak of Kilimanjaro-Uhuru Peak. This landscape resembles Scotland more than it does tropical Africa, with mossy rocks and trickles of water streaming between tufts of grass. At this height, the mountain has its own weather system. The winds blow in a different direction up here, and when it hits the mountain face, an instant storm can occur, or the clouds can suddenly open up to the stars and sky, surrounded by a carpet of clouds from the different weather patterns below. The next landscape is the alpine desert. It is barren with nothing more than rocks and snow around. At this stage in the climb, it is advisable to eat simple foods like congee or porridge, and wear warm clothes as the night temperatures average around negative 10 degrees Celsius[75]. The final landscape is permanent snow, which looks like a scene from Antarctica.

At the summit, the trekker is on the edge of the Kilimanjaro volcanic crater. To one side are permanent glaciers off in the distance sitting amongst a sulphur pit at the volcano's centre. Turning around at this point and looking back in the direction of travel, the African planes open out with Mount Meru, the next volcano in the chain, off in the distance. (See Figure 26: Mount Kilimanjaro, Tanzania.)

Figure 26: Mount Kilimanjaro, Tanzania.

The other landmark to meet this, and only this category is Mount Everest. It is the tallest mountain in the world located in Nepal and China with the border running across its summit. It is three kilometres taller than Mount Kilimanjaro. The journey to the top is well documented with trekkers attempting the climb since Edmund Hillary first reached the summit in 1953. Of course, his porter Tenzing Norgay was there too, and equally deserving of the title of first.

In 2019, the PBS News Hour reported, *"Overcrowding on Mount Everest contributes to rise in deaths."*[76] The photo in the article shows a mountain peak in the distance with a line of red, orange, black and blue padded polyester hooded jackets pressed together like people are waiting to get into a night club. Eleven people died in that season. The article goes on to say, *"Because of the altitude, climbers have just hours to reach the top before they are at risk of a pulmonary edema, when the lungs fill with liquid."*[76]

That year saw 381 permits granted to climb the peak and accompanied by many more of Nepal's ethnic Sherpa community as porters. In 2014 an avalanche caused the death of 16 Sherpa guides. China, which believes all the mountain is in its territory, also runs treks up the northern side of the mountain, and both sides are littered with empty oxygen canisters, food packaging and other debris.

It is a shame that the race for climbing the highest mountain only allows for one winner, Mount Everest. Yet, a race for climbing the greatest mountain could be for Kilimanjaro, or it could be for Cradle Mountain in Tasmania, which meets seven of UNESCO's ten criteria. There is also the iconic shaped Matterhorn in Switzerland, Mount Fuji in Japan, the historic Mount Vesuvius in Italy or Mount Sinai in Egypt. All these destinations are worthy of attention, yet our blinded attraction to the tallest, and ignorance of the other spectacular places of natural and cultural meaning causes a dangerous level of over-tourism and prevents other mountain communities from thriving.

Natural Significance

Criterion (viii), *"To be outstanding examples representing major stages of earth's history, including the record of life, significant on-going geological processes in the development of landforms, significant geomorphic or physiographic features."*[64]

Mount Etna in Italy is the best representation of this category. It is the only landmark that Lonely Planet[6] and List Challenge[77] contribute to the meta bucket list of landmarks, that fit this criterion. The mountain is an active volcano that erupted as recently as 2018. In 2017 it injured ten people and in 1987 two tourists were killed. If you ever see video footage of a volcano erupting it is probably Etna, she can be both dangerous and photogenic.

This criterion has a few volcanos, nearly all are extinct having erupted tens of thousands of years ago. There are some craters, caves and fossil pits, which, strictly speaking, are not landmarks as they do not fit the standard laid out earlier. I do feel Lena Pillars Nature Park in Russia is worth mentioning. The park cannot be strictly defined as a landmark as it is a riverbank cliff only seen from one side of the river and is a series of stone, vertical pillars, rather than a single landmark object. Yet it is impressive. It reminds me of the movie *Lord of the Rings* when the small hobbits leave the battlefield and go into the mighty Fangorn Forest. The pillars lining this rocky riverbank appear as gigantic trees amongst green grass (pine trees). They are staggered like trees in a forest. Each pillar is the size of a high-rise building. If you view the cliff from the air, the optical illusion gets discovered, revealing that the pillars are on a sloping bank with the ground height equal to the top of the pillars. The land does not disappear to the horizon; it slopes up the cliff face giving the appearance that it may go on forever. (See Figure 27.)

In Hubei Province, China, two national parks fit this criterion for their natural plant and animal life. The region is known for the Clouded Leopard, Chinese Giant Salamander, the Golden Snub-nosed Monkey, Common Leopard, and the Asian Black Bear. The area covers 73,000 hectares, therefore, is not a landmark, but within the Shennongjia Forestry District, a human-made landmark feature is like no other. The Shennong Altar is for worshipping the Emperor of the Five Grains who was a legendary ruler of China. The altar is located through manicured gardens and up steps on the mountainside. At the top, clouded in incense, is a cylindrical grey stone statue towering above the height of the trees. There is a face carved into the upper portions with two horns on either side standing out horizontally tripling the width of the statue. The mountains around the altar are naturally beautiful with steep sheer cliffs amongst a vertical forest growing up their steep slopes. (See Figure 28: The Shennong Altar.)

Figure 27: Lina Pillars, Russia.

Many of the entrants fitting this more geological and landform category, also meet the next criterion on life processes.

Natural Processes
Criterion (ix), *"To be outstanding examples representing significant on-going ecological and biological processes in the evolution and development of terrestrial, fresh water, coastal and marine ecosystems and communities of plants and animals."*[64]

Notable in this category is Mount Kenya, which is the second-highest peak in Africa after Mount Kilimanjaro and the Three Sisters in the Blue Mountains just outside of Sydney, Australia. They are a series of three stone pillars on the edge of a forested valley.

Figure 28: The Shennong Altar.

Nature Conservation

Criterion (x), *"To contain the most important and significant natural habitats for in-situ conservation of biological diversity, including those containing threatened species of outstanding universal value from the point of view of science or conservation."*[64]

The final category is less about landmarks and more about large nature conservation areas. Angel Falls in Venezuela is a landmark that fits this criterion and the three other natural feature criteria of vii, viii and ix. The falls are the highest uninterrupted waterfall in the world, directly descending 979 metres – close to a kilometre drop. It begins at the higher planes of the Auyán-tepui Mountain, down a rock bluff to the river Rio Kerepacupai Meru valley below. It is one of

Venezuela's top tourist attractions even though it is in an isolated jungle with the only access via boat, which is an interesting experience.

UNESCO Winners

There are two landmarks that achieve the highest rating by attaining seven out of the ten UNESCO World Heritage criteria. The first is Cradle Mountain in Australia's Tasmanian wilderness. The certification statement is as follows,

"In a region that has been subjected to severe glaciation, these parks and reserves, with their steep gorges, covering an area of over 1 million hectares, constitute one of the last expanses of temperate rainforest in the world. Remains found in limestone caves attest to the human occupation of the area for more than 20,000 years."[78]

The second is Mount Taishan in China, with its temple at the top of the mountain accessed to by 6,666 steps, climbing 1400 metres.

"The sacred Mount Tai ('shan' means 'mountain') was the object of an imperial cult for nearly 2,000 years, and the artistic masterpieces found there are in perfect harmony with the natural landscape. It has always been a source of inspiration for Chinese artists and scholars and symbolizes ancient Chinese civilizations and beliefs."[79]

These two examples are both winners in the race for meaning by exhibiting natural qualities, which include plant, animal, and geological rarities, as well as a rich cultural history. Yet they are relatively both unknown as landmarks. Their fame is lacking, with both in need of better interpretation tools to make them more understandable to the general public.

Having meaning alone does not make a landmark great. If the visitor is unable to understand the experience, then their value is lost. Interpretation of cultural and natural assets then becomes essential for a landmark to be considered significant in our world. If a visitor to Cradle Mountain or Mount Taishan never learns the value of their visit, the landmark is less likely to receive attention and is unlikely to move forward in the landmark race.

Furthermore, how visitors remember a location then becomes crucial in raising the status of a landmark in the landmark race. Memory plays an essential role in how we understand and communicate a landmark, and the physical shape of the landmark can help make it more memorable.

8. The Race to be Memorable

"...the Architect is the keeper of civilisations."
Goldberger [80]

Great Architecture

Architecture is often considered a form of non-verbal language and can be thought of in a similar way to spoken languages. Experts in the language of architecture have a very different reading of a building compared to someone who only knows a few words of the lexicon. The notion of an architectural language has been around for a while with the books, *The Language of Post Modern Architecture* by Charles Jencks[81] and *The Classical Language of Architecture* by John Summerson[82], both translating the nuances of the language to everyone.

To take this analogy further, let us consider how a child compares with the renowned architect Frank Lloyd Wright when reading the Big Orange – the abandoned round orange coloured ball from Chapter 6. The child would run up the path excited to see the Orange, yet the architect would see it as less thought-provoking past the initial reading.

What if we compare this to the house design of *Fallingwater*, a UNESCO World Heritage site designed by Wright in Pennsylvania, USA, that is considered a piece of great architecture. The architect would spend hours discussing the design and the experiences it features. The child would glance at the house for a moment and then spend the afternoon playing in the creek below. The child is yet to learn the language of architecture, and gains little from the experience. Even for many adults, the language can escape them.

If we all learnt the language of architecture when young, the landmark race would simply be a race for beautiful architecture. As Paul Goldberger, in the book, *Why Architecture Matters*, states,

"Beauty is that which cannot be changed except for the worst. A beautiful building is one which nothing can be added, and nothing can be taken away."[80]

Adding and taking away of design is best demonstrated by the construction of the Sagrada Familia, Barcelona's Cathedral designed by Antonian Gaudi, which began construction in 1882 and is still under construction today (estimated to be complete in 2026). Gaudi, possessed with *adding* to the cathedral, stepped back onto the street to view his design and was hit by a streetcar. He was dressed so poorly the hospital considered him homeless. His obsession with the building had given him little time for clothing and probably hygiene. The cathedral is ranked as the second greatest landmark in the meta bucket list and stands as proof that the race to be *great* can be won by great architecture. It has received the most positive comments on TripAdvisor of all landmarks and is the foremost driver for tourism to the city. If a location wishes to win the landmark race, then all it needs to do is to get an architect to give up their life for their design and have buildings under construction for over 138 years.

This extreme devotion to creating a landmark is not possible for most architects and is not essentially necessary to win the race, although it can help.

Not everyone knows the language of architecture. It is a knowledge held by the architectural elite and those with large university debts. So what about the child's opinion of the Big Orange and the house Fallingwater? It is elitist to ignore the child's opinion, and the opinion of billions of other people who do not understand the language of architecture.

If we take a broader approach to landmarks, looking at how they are understood by everyone rather than a deeper intellectual approach, we get a different outcome. The results then mirror visitor numbers, reflect rental incomes, and align with property values. It also shows us what people appreciate and matches the tourist experience of having an enjoyable time visiting a landmark. In a broader approach to the language, we can break it down to understand why some landmarks work and why some do not. We may even discover what triggers an architect to say to their child, *"What the hell, I do want to see the Big Orange too. Let's go!"*

Before we move on, great architecture and work by the great architects are covered in the section on *meaning*. The UNESCO World Heritage criteria (i) and (iv) both review and rate the works of great architects. Yet for a landmark to be significant in an inclusive, general public sense, it also needs to be remarkable and memorable to everyone, not just architects.

The Memorable

In understanding the greatness of landmarks, it is useful to know how memorable it is. Structures, and even natural features that are memorable to everyone is less about the field of architecture and more into the areas of sociology and urban design. The field of memory and landmarks is incredibly extensive with a great deal of research going into how computers perceive and identify a landmark (urban features) for navigation of driverless cars. The root of this research comes from the field of urban design with Kevin Lynch, John Myer and Donald Appleyard setting up the basis to this work. In 1969, Appleyard[83] conducted a series of studies that measured how memorable building features are. His team tested how easily the general public recalled these landmarks based on the following assessment tools, ranked by importance:

First- Surface: The most memorable factor of a building is the façade. Bright colours, an ornate façade, and different materials all add to its memorability factor.

Second- Use Intensity: If a building has a multitude of uses (also known as mixed-use), then this increases the likelihood that a building will be remembered.

Third- Movement: People are attracted to other people. Jane Jacobs, a non-theoretical urban designer, observed this fact when she noticed people crowded into an urban plaza, leaving a large open park deserted nearby. People remember a popular place, one that has people coming and going, or even a place with people standing around drinking.

Equal Fourth- Use Singularity: People find important how the use of a building differs from those around it. A church, for example, will be remembered in a residential neighbourhood. The opposite is also true in a street of churches – the only apartment block is more likely to be remembered.

Equal Fourth- Size: The size of a building is equally as important as the last category. The notion from chapter 5 The Race for Tall, that size is valued is acknowledged here, but it is less important than the above factors. A big building is more likely to be forgotten if a noisy bar is across the road.

Equal Fourth- Viewpoint Significance: As a person travels, whether by car or walking, buildings in their eyeline will be noticed far more than those off to the side. Urban designers often design cities to set up major view lines to important buildings as a response to this. Canberra, Washington, and Brasilia are all examples of cities designed this way.

Seventh- Shape: The complexity of a building's shape is the next factor that contributes to how memorable a building is. If a structure is box-like and straightforward in shape, it is less likely to be remembered. If it has many different faces, forms, and surfaces (known as articulation in the Town Planning field), then it will be remembered.

Eighth- Contour: Contour is how it stands out next to its neighbour. If a building forms part of a row, with the same building height, it is less likely to be remembered. If it stands alone, for example, three storeys in a grassy field, then it is more likely to be remembered.

The ranking of these factors in order of importance helps us understand what urban design factors make a landmark great. All elements have a very similar weight, only varying 10% from each other. Other factors analysed in the study were concluded to be significantly less critical; for example, the quality of a building. It was found that quality tends to be a neighbourhood scale factor and not based on individual buildings. Disappointingly for advertisers, signs were also found to be considerably less memorable.

When this analysis is added to the list of great landmarks, we get only one that exhibits all the best of these qualities.

Mont Saint Michel. On top of a column standing at 170 metres in France, is the white statue of Saint Michael with a sword in one hand raised to the sky, two wings splayed each side like an angel and a halo, similar to the Statue of Liberty's, behind his helmet. He looks down on the landmark island of Mont Saint Michel off the coast of Normandy. This walled town sits in the mudflats of the river Couesnon. At low tide, it looks like it is in a desert, while at high tide, it stands surrounded by the sea and protected from invaders. The island is tall and rocky with a low and robust wall built around the water's edge to protect it from cannon fire. There are houses with prominent chimneys, all climbing up the hill with spaces for trees to push up between the buildings. Small pedestrian laneways are the only routes to the top with the Cathedral of Saint Michel at its apex. The statue of Saint Michel stands at the highest point of the cathedral's spire. The island looks medieval and paranoid out in the mudflats. Pilgrims who once travelled to the island needed to time their arrival with the tides. They would need to sprint across the mudflats to avoid the rising sea from engulfing them. Mont Saint Michel is isolated from the world and is so prominent compared to the flat ocean. It is genuinely a great landmark. Its surface patterns are a mixture of foliage, rock and brickwork with windows and roofs. It only has a population of thirty people but swells to two million visitors a year, all linked to the mainland by a new bridge that now provides 24-hour access to the town. (See Figure 29: Mont Saint Michel.)

Figure 29: Mont Saint Michel.

Bridges rate highly on the memorable scale and frequently appear in the list, with the Golden Gate Bridge equal second on the memorable scale, shared with eight other landmarks. It has a distinctive red colour, not gold, unlike its name, and links from the north of San Francisco to Marin County in California. The American Society of Engineers declared it as one of the modern wonders of the world, which does sound a tad biased. It is over two and a half kilometres long and made of steel. It has a flat freeway deck suspended from cables that create an arc stretched between two towers, 227 metres high.

Tower Bridge in London also ranks second on the memorable scale. It is often confused with London Bridge; the actual London bridge is located up the river and appears as an unremarkable 1970s concrete bridge. Tower Bridge has two castle-shaped towers connected at the top by a metal span, and a draw bridge in the centre just above the waterline. This bridge is distinctively London and has served as an icon of the city since its construction in 1894. (See Figure 30.)

Figure 30: Tower Bridge, London.

An architecturally fascinating building that appears in equal second place on the scale is the Guggenheim Museum in Bilbao. The city had always been unknown to most outside of Spain, with the capital, Madrid, the famous Barcelona, Valencia, and Seville all having significantly larger populations. Bilbao lacked the uniqueness of these other cities. In 1991 the Solomon R. Guggenheim Foundation, with headquarters in New York and through funding by the local Basque Government, built the museum in the disused docklands of the city. Frank Gehry and his team designed a building that appears as a pile of paper streamers made from reflective titanium with sections of the building constructed with beige limestone. This building put Bilbao on the international stage, receiving visitors from all around the globe. In its first few years, it attracted four million tourists and generated 500 million euros.

Appearing at the bottom of the memorable scale with a score of 6.14 is Vinson Massif. A massif is a geological term used to describe a group of mountains that are a result of the movement of the Earth's crust. Mount Vinson is the highest peak in Antarctica and is part of the Massif. Understandably, this landmark's rate is low when you consider that it is in one of the least most active places in the world and has the surface pattern of only snow.

The system used here to score how memorable a landmark is also helping us understand how unique it is in its local environment. Being memorable does not measure how beautiful or wonderful the landmark is.

A building that is ugly and hated can still be highly memorable.

From Hate to Great

Around two hundred years ago the French Revolution gave way to an empire under the rule of Napoleon I. After losing the Hundred Days War the nation saw Louis XVI's brothers come to power with what was to become known of as the Bourbon Restoration. The July Revolution in 1830 saw Louis Philippe d'Orléans take control of the nation and he would remain in power for the next eighteen years.

Meanwhile, the rural area of Côte-d'Or in Dijon, a typical agricultural town of the time, was experiencing a different revolution that was shared throughout Europe. It was the Industrial Revolution, and it would eventually change the world forever.

François Boenickhausen and his wife Catherine Moneuse, on the 15th of December 1832, were not concerned with the revolutions going on around them. Catherine was busy giving birth to her first child Gustave. Over the coming months, François had to leave his job as an army administrator to support Catherine in child-rearing and running her successful coal delivery company. Catherine used her knowledge of timer trading from her family's business to develop a charcoal company. The company was so successful she needed François to help with both family and work life. It was not long before Catherine was back running the business and her mother came in to help raise Gustave. She was not known as a pleasant woman, and although she was blind, she managed to control Gustave with a stick. Gustave respected his mother, with her significant achievements and joked that his grandmother used to hit him, but it was never that hard.

Gustave grew up in the town, and in 1852 passed his exams at the École Centrale where he specialised in chemistry. His dream was to take over his uncle's business and was close to succeeding when his father, François, bought the political revolution discussion into the family. The family split due to a resulting argument – his uncle was a republican and François supported Napoleon. With his chemistry path blocked, Gustave decided to turn to metalwork and started working for the railway engineer Charles Nepveu.

The business was struggling, and Gustave kept working for him even though he was not getting paid. When the company was absorbed by the larger Compagnie Générale des Chemins de Fers, his precision and enjoyment of challenges had earnt him the project to design the Bordeaux Bridge at the age of only 25. It was during this time he experimented with various construction techniques that would help him later in life.

His career began taking off with the boom of the Industrial Revolution and the use of iron and steel as a new, more robust building material. It was around the 1880s when Gustave dropped his father's last name of Boenickhausen. The family were known as Boenickhausen of the Eifel mountains, where his father, François, had immigrated from. Gustave was now in control of the business, and he changed his name, and the company's name, to the now-famous name of Gustave Eiffel.

It was around this time when Gustave Eiffel would work on one of the grand landmarks of the world. Can you guess which one? It was the Statue of Liberty.

The sculptor Bartholdi, to celebrate the centenary of the United States of America's independence, had decided to build a giant statue to stand in New York Harbor. The work to date had been carried out by the architect Eugène Viollet-Le-Duc who passed away, leaving the project unfinished. Gustave took over the skeletal component of the project with his company designing and building the supports for the large interlocking copper plates that were to adorn the statue.

Meanwhile, in Paris, Maurice Koechlin and Emile Nouguier, were discussing the construction of a tower to be at the centrepiece of the 1889 World Exposition. Once the architect Stephen Sauvestre added embellishments to the engineered tower, Gustave begun to support the project and financed 80% of the cost in exchange for receiving entry profits for twenty years.

In 1885, Gustave was reported as saying, in relation to the positive qualities of the tower, that it would symbolise, *"...not only the art of the modern engineer, but also the century of Industry and Science in which we are living, and for which the way was prepared by the great scientific movement of the eighteenth century and by the Revolution of 1789, to which this monument will be built as an expression of France's gratitude."*[84]

In 1886, a competition was conducted for the design of a landmark with the rules modified to make their scheme the winner. Gustave would name the tower after his company and himself.

Construction began on the Eiffel Tower in 1887, and everyone hated it.

Newspapers received a deluge of angry letters with the famous poet, Guy de Maupassant, declaring that he always ate his lunch at the base of the tower because it was the only place in Paris where he could look out and not see it[85]. An organisation called the *Committee of Three Hundred* was formed by prominent Parisian artists, painters, and writers to stop the construction of the tower.

"For every single foot that was supposed to be erected, there was one displeased Parisian who was offended

by the notion and protested against the construction of this useless and monstrous Eiffel Tower."[85]

Over time the tower was at first tolerated, and with the gathering of tourists, all wishing to view Paris from its apex, it was accepted. Today it is loved. The Eiffel Tower became something that is uniquely French and a symbol of Paris. To take away the tower would destroy the global image of the city.

The Eiffel Tower is so prominent in Paris; its memorable factors push emotions to the extremes of being loved or hated.

The concept of how a landmark can go from being hated to loved, played out in my home city of Melbourne. Sculptor Ron Robertson-Swann produced a huge, bright yellow, folding triangular sculpture for the revamped square in the city centre. The design of this square utilised the local bluestone, a drab and depressing stone that covered the ground, walls, and undersides of bridges amongst a maze of fountains. This bright yellow feature stuck out amongst the stone backdrop and was instantly despised.

Queen Elizabeth II opened the square and seeing the sculpture suggested that maybe it could be painted "a more agreeable colour"[86]. It was not long before the sculpture was removed and placed on the river in a 1970s-styled featureless park opposite abandoned wharves next to an overhead railway. It sat there for years; graffiti built upon its faces, and skateboards would chip away at its hard edges as the city slowly forgot about it. At the end of the 1990s, the river was to be revitalised with the construction of a $650 million Crown Casino complex. It had ballrooms, conference facilities and five-star restaurants all looking out to the river, all would see the sculpture decaying on the other side. It had to be moved again.

In 2002 a new site was chosen in the industrial area a few streets back from the river[87]. I worked on the design of this streetscape back when I was a graduate. Grant Street had to be removed to make way for a freeway tunnel underneath it. It was then put back in a process known as 'cut and cover'. Because the street was built on top of a tunnel, trees were planted in containers and would only grow to the size of large shrubs. The buildings to be built along this street had to be set back from the road to prevent breaching the tunnel. This made for a long park along one side of the street giving the sculpture a large space where no trees could grow to hide it.

As the new millennium moved on, the precinct became an arts precinct due to the National Gallery of Victoria and its bluestone façade being only a block away. Growth of the Victoria College of the Arts, National Institute of Performing Arts occurred in the early part of the new century, all began to surround the sculpture. When the Australian Centre for Contemporary Art was developed just behind it, the sculpture stood as a feature element to its street front.

The landscape even mimics its triangular form, and the architecture of the centre was similar in shape. The city loves the sculpture titled The Vault now, graffiti is removed within an hour of application (this is serious for a city that prides itself on its graffiti art form) and it stands as a Southbank landmark. Its old home of the City Square was removed. The park opposite the casino still looks like a 1970s park with nothing done, but the Vault is a glowing yellow feature in the centre of an Arts Precinct where students can relax in its shade between classes.

Landmarks that are unique and memorable, but were hated when first built, tends to be a common occurrence. Some others are:

Guggenheim Museum, New York: Designed by Frank Lloyd Wright, many artists scorned the building feeling the structure overpowered the art inside. The building is now a world icon.

The Empire State Building, New York: The building was seen by many as an indulgent waste of money built too far from proper public transit links. It was known as the 'Empty State Building' due to its lack of occupancy when built.

Sagrada Familia, Barcelona: George Orwell described it as *"One of the most hideous buildings in the world"* and remarked that the anarchists of Spain's civil war showed, *"bad taste in not blowing it up"*[88]. Salvador Dalí spoke of its *"terrifying and edible beauty"* and

Pablo Picasso wished those responsible for it would be *"sent to hell"*. It is now one of the most popular attractions in the world.

The Pompidou Centre, Paris: Appearing like it is under construction, with scaffolding around the outside, the centre is designed to show the workings of the building on the outside. Meanwhile, the inside is kept simple and roomy.

Vittorio Emanuele II Monument, Rome: Completing construction in 1935 the monument is in honour of the first king of unified Italy. Locals gave it the nicknames of "the typewriter", "false teeth", and "wedding cake", due to its classic roman columns arranged in an arch resembling as critiqued, false teeth. Yet tourists love it and visit it in droves.

A Tale of Two Circles

Two circular landmarks were opened on the 31st of December 1999. The London Eye, a temporary large Ferris wheel was constructed on the banks of the River Thames. Further downstream on the Greenwich Peninsular was the Millennium Dome, ninth largest building in the world, built as an exhibition centre. Both were created to celebrate the beginning of the third millennium.

The London Eye was built to last only five years and is a technological, futuristic landmark that contrasts considerably with the old historic buildings of London. It looks across to Big Ben and the Houses of Parliament and cantilevers out onto the river. It was a temporary structure in celebration of the date and Londoners enjoyed the opportunity to see their city from a great height. It was a rare experience at the time due to building height restrictions across the city. It was instantly loved. The tourists flooded into the city to see it before it was removed. It is now the most popular paid attraction in the United Kingdom.

The Millennium Dome was to be a permanent exhibition space with a white dome structure supported by a ring of yellow towers that protruded like candles from a cake. The towers had cables that supported the roof, allowing the inside to be free of columns. It was instantly hated.

The original exhibition attracted half the visitors it was expected to draw, causing it to become a highly political issue. The newspapers at the time had headlines like, *"The Black Hole of Stratford East"* and *"The £758m disaster zone"*[89]. The architect Richard Rogers who was behind the design, said in 2015 that it, *"Couldn't have had a worse reception if you'd worked hard to deliberately upset everybody"*.

Both landmarks were follies to mark the calendar. Arguably the Millennium Dome was still more useful than a wheel that just goes around and around. Yet the Dome was used for the 2012 Summer Olympics for the artistic gymnastics' events, and the medal rounds of basketball.

This comparison, and some previous examples, point to a key factor in getting significant landmarks built. If the landmark is to be too memorable and too shocking for people to accept, then declaring the landmark a temporary structure goes a long way in dismissing the initial shock of a unique structure being built in our cities.

Many landmarks were temporary structures including the Eiffel tower, which was so shocking even for its temporariness could not deflect its hatred. If it is stated as temporary and is successful, it will be retained, and if it gets removed, then possibly it should not have been built in the first place. It seems people need to have enough time to get used to something truly unique. It could be argued the London Eye's uniqueness rebranded the city from a boring old European city to one that is both old and new. The London Eye paved the way for the new landmark buildings of 30 St Mary Axe (Swiss Re or Gherkin building) and the Shard tower, all iconic new structures in a historic city, that was previously too old to change.

To make a landmark temporary is the most potent tool designers have in creating a unique and bold landmark that avoids criticism. The Hollywood sign was temporary. If a landmark is loved, it will stay; if it is hated, then it will go. Furthermore, this is factually true for all architecture, buildings get demolished all the time. If they are loved, they get heritage status and stay forever. If hated, they get knocked down to make way for something else. So why not state this upfront and deflect all criticism? Design the wildest landmark ever seen and tell everyone it is just for ten years.

The Race for Second

The problems with designing buildings that are unique and memorable without the public criticism that follows, is a challenge for all great designs. So why take on that battle? Why not strive for second place instead? Many landmarks do.

Appearing first on the list of the greatest landmarks, based on popularity and notoriety, cultural value and by its height, we have the fore mentioned Eiffel Tower. The Tower contrasts greatly to other buildings in Paris, being tall, a light structure, unique in the use of metal rather than the masonry typical in the city. Its age, being built in 1887, is also an outstanding quality that other landmarks do not get to enjoy. So why try to beat it? Why not just come second to it?

Sir John Bickerstaffe, a former mayor of the coastal town of Blackpool in England's north-west, decided to do precisely that. He visited the World's Fair in Paris in 1889, the central feature was the Eiffel Tower. Returning to his home in the vacation town, he put the gears in motion to produce a similar tower standing at 158 metres, half the height of its French counterpart. It was only four years after the Paris Fair when the Blackpool Tower opened. Tourists paid sixpence for admission and sixpence more for a ride in the lift to the top. The first members of the public to ascend the tower had been local journalists in September 1893, during construction and had to use ladders. Its height was so significant that when the top caught fire, it was seen from 80 kilometres away[90].

Sir Bickerstaffe was not the only person inspired by the World's Fair. Two other towers began construction a few years later in 1891. One, the Petřín Lookout Tower, which stands at one-sixth the size of the Eiffel Tower in Prague, and the other is Watkin's Tower in Wembley London. Watkin's Tower was to be 34 metres higher than the Eiffel Tower, yet the company went into liquidation. The completed section had to be dynamited to bring it down for safety reasons.

The race for second-best Eiffel Tower boomed along throughout the 1900s with replicas built around the world. It was not until 1958 when Tokyo built its tower eight metres taller than its French cousin. Looking remarkably different in red and white (so it is more visible to aircraft), and a solid mesh rather than the four pylons we know from the Eiffel Tower, it was built primarily for TV broadcast. Today it brings in hundreds of thousands of people as a tourist attraction to its observation deck.

China breached the Tokyo Tower's height in 1999 with construction of the Dragon Tower in Harbin City. The tower is more multi-sided than four-sided like its predecessor and is used for television transmission and has an observation deck.

Some more blatant attempts for second place appear in Las Vegas and Macau with the casino induced 'Paris Las Vegas' and 'Parisian Macao'. Both are half the size of the Eiffel Tower and tempt tourists with the question- *'Why go to Paris when you have a tower right here? Oh... and gamble, you have to gamble too.'*

Replicas get a free ride when it comes to making landmarks. The Eiffel Tower was new and revolutionary, yet it was hated at the beginning. Over time people got used to it, then they loved it. Now nothing is more Parisian. Yet its copies never had to contend with the hate. It is challenging for someone to describe something revolutionary and new and still get it built. It is far easier for someone to say, *'we're going to build one of those, but we will do it here.'*

As a designer, it seems counter-intuitive that the replication of an existing landmark would have a positive outcome. Does the world need more Eiffel Towers or Large Buddhas? Based on the list of great landmarks, it seems the answer to this is yes. Yes, it does, and the more, the better. Replication of landmarks of meaning seems a perfectly valid way to attract attention. It seems more successful than replicating a large version of a pineapple or an orange. Somehow these replicas manage to copy some of its awe and some of its distinctiveness, although in a smaller dose. The large statues also capture this by replicating the values of the person or god they represent and incorporate those values into the structure, making them popular in the landmark race. They can never win the race, but they can rate pretty high, which is not so bad.

9. The Opinion List

"I am entitled to my opinion." Karen meme.

The meta bucket list of great landmarks is assembled from books and online articles from travel writers and everyday people from around the world. These are opinions. *The Lonely Planet*'s Top 500 list was sourced from their travel writers' experiences and voted on by people in the Lonely Planet community[6]. List Challenge is a website that allows the general public to add to the list and vote on what landmarks they deem to be the greatest in the world[77]. There are the *Architectural Digest*'s opinions of the world's greatest landmarks[91], *Hello Magazine*'s top twelve[92] and a TripAdvisor Top Attractions list, to name a few. When all these landmarks are placed in a list, it is over 400 entries long. This was to become the base of the research. Although many significant landmarks were not nominated in any online lists, they were added and then tested to see if they ranked high in the analysis. Around two thousand were added, and they all fell below the previous four hundred due to their lack of fame and low popularity scores. The reason for this is because the Great Landmarks List is a sociological list based on people's ideas of what is considered excellent, and not about the hidden or unknown landmarks that are overlooked.

As a result, the added landmarks were less known for a good reason. Some had limitations of access; for example, landmarks in North Korea, while others were not a landmark at all, such as Ajanta Caves in Maharashtra, India; a cave cannot be a landmark. Rolled into this list were also ratings given to the landmark based on positive comments from TripAdvisor. TripAdvisor is useful as ratings are across language groups. However, it is biased towards travellers who are likely to comment on that website. In the ranking score it is only given minimal weighting to help differentiate between landmarks that have the same ranking.

Opinions, in this online age are everywhere. There is a belief today that every person's opinion is valid. Even the great landmarks are subject to this. The Sagrada Familia is one of the greatest landmarks in the world, attracting so many tourists to Barcelona that the city is breaking under the tourism pressure. The landmark has the most positive comments on TripAdvisor dwarfing the Colosseum, which is at number two, by over 16,000 statements noting it to be 'excellent' or at least 'very good.'

Negative comments are ignored when creating an opinion rating, with the few negative comments typically based on disappointment of a tour company or ticketing. The rating is to find positive opinions and to compare them across landmarks and not negative sentiments.

Still, some negative opinions are gems that show the diversity of how people think. Some of the most astonishing comments on the Sagrada Familia are as follows:

*"**A desert in a cathedral** - Gaudi's folly: if only he'd been given something functional to design, like Montaner's glorious hospital or concert hall. His houses are wonderful, but as a sacred place of worship this is simply absurd, especially now that it is being voraciously exploited for fast bucks. This was my worst mass tourism experience since the Vatican and I would not recommend it to anyone: the interior reminded me of a Scottish discotheque in the 1980s and offered a similar sense of spirituality..."* SJWilson, TripAdvisor[93]

*"**Overrated and ugly** - ... as soon as we emerged from the metro and had the displeasure of viewing this eyesore we did a quick 180 and headed home. disgusting. the silver lining was the cranes in the background of this church. they were a welcoming sight - anything to avert your attention from what I can only describe as a monstrosity."* Tom Vaughan, TripAdvisor[93]

*"**Designed by LSD** - ...In no way does it represent anything Christian. We love architecture and found

nothing to love here. Packed with people who came to take selfies to check it off their bucket list... My humble opinion of those that gave it a great review felt obligated or were afraid of eternal damnation [if] they said anything negative..." travelerLittleTownSc, TripAdvisor

"This is the ugliest building I've ever seen in my 80 years." Safari602564, TripAdvisor[93]

"butter dissapointment [sic]" theopipis, Tripadvisor[93]

"Hideous monstrosity that's a testament to all that's wrong with the church! *- ... [It] Is a seriously hideous looking building that is ugly from every angle. As much as I like some of Gaudi's work I have to say this looks like something a person who placed last in a cake decorating competition got to decorate..."* Simon-from-Adelaide, TripAdvisor[93]

"Ugly *- This is the ugliest building I have ever seen. Still can't see what others see. There are so many beautiful cathedrals through[out] Spain and the world that put this building to shame."* Beth1229, TripAdvisor[93]

Clients

Urban designers, planners and architects all listen to other people's opinions when designing, with the client's view holding the most weight. I have seen months of work trashed by a CEO who looks at a plan for two minutes, turns and says, "I don't like it."

It is common for a client to say, *"It needs more something."* I have heard, it needs to be more 'Swedish', in China from a Chinese client. More *'exciting'* that has stumped the design team for months. Often different colour trees on the plan will resolve this. Then there is the common, *'taller'*, *'longer'*, *'more water'*, *'less water'* or in urban design, like a throwback to the 1970s, *'It needs to be curvy.'*

The Public
When dealing with governments and councils, we go through a public consultation process. The process involves meeting with the community, key non-government groups, utility providers or the entire general public. It is done in many ways. There are *roadshows* where the team will set up in locations all around the suburb with drawings and reports. They will sit down and do a questionnaire with open questions like, *'what do you think of this?'*

The most enjoyable experiences I have had, is the 'Enquiry by Design' process. Community leaders and interested people gather for a morning presentation about the site and the project aims. The afternoon is spent with everyone designing the scheme in groups, all putting in what they think is best. That night the design team stays behind, and so often end up working all night to produce three schemes that incorporate different ideas and present it back to everyone in the morning. The group votes on the best scheme and all new comments are recorded for further development of the chosen plan.

This process is useful in many ways. It brings people along for the design ride, enabling them to appreciate the weighing up of different conflicting ideas. It forces participants to express their opinion now or 'forever hold their peace'. I have seen this argument used where a participant said a week later that they did not like the scheme the group produced in a follow-up meeting. They were scolded for their lack of initiative in speaking up during the workshop, and the opinion was ignored. This process is also helpful when there are language difficulties. Designers can use the international language of drawing to communicate across barriers, and I have experienced heated discussions using drawings with teams from around the world, with each team unable to speak the other's language.

The design product that comes out of this process is rarely one of *greatness*. It is always a sensible, expected design with no surprises. The most exciting design I have ever seen come out of an Enquiry by Design process was a Park in Northala Fields in London. A council-owned, old industrial area was to be turned into a park. The concept was to use waste soil and concrete rubble from construction sites in central London and charge a fee for them to be dumped on the site. The payments generated income for the construction of the park. The residents had gotten the opinion that this was a bad idea. It was thought the site was to be a dump or tip, and they initially tried to stop the project. In the design session, we asked what people wanted in the new park. The conversation went like this:

"A fishing lake."

"I want the lake to be for model boating."

"No, they will scare the fish, we can't have that."

"We should have wetlands." Added another person

"No, the plants will disrupt the boats."

"What about full-sized rowboats." Added a new voice to the group.

Finally, my director at the time interjected, sounding like Oprah Winfrey in a car giveaway, *"How about you get a lake for fishing and you get a lake for model boats, you can have one for rowboats and we all can have lakes for wetlands."*

It was not long before everyone in the room's wishes for the site had their idea incorporated into the design. The park now has ten lakes and four gigantic cone-shaped hills that stand as landmarks along the A40 freeway. The larger the cones, the higher the revenue. It was one of the few design projects I know where everybody won. The council did not have to fund the project, construction waste removal companies got a dumping location close to their sites, speeding up their excavation, and the residents all obtained a park they wanted.

Public consultation, whether it is with the community, clients, or other stakeholders (stakeholders are utilities, tourism operators, local businesses, anyone who has a stake in the project), is a process practised in most countries for big projects. Furthermore, consultation is not just for the design sphere; movie producers consult with a test screening audience to get a handle on public opinion too. Marketing people conduct surveys, and so do politicians. There is a movement in political circles for informed public consultation where a group representing parts of society are brought together, like a jury trial, to hear all the professional evidence to decide based on the detailed evidence.

There are two broad issues with public consultation that are a challenge designers face when listening to opinions of landmarks.

1. How do we weigh opinions compared to other factors?
2. How do we deal with outlier opinions that go against the norm?

These dilemmas have plagued the public consultation process over the years. Recently it has been sociology and the rise of big data who have found the answers. The more data gathered, the outliers, the opinions outside general sentiment, are ignored if not needed. This way of understanding design is new to the industry and is becoming a significant force in architecture, urban design, and planning.

Evidence-Based Design

Design exists in the realm between science and art. Many designers today work under the theory of Phenomenology. The Stanford Encyclopedia of Philosophy lists it as:

"Phenomenology is the study of structures of consciousness as experienced from the first-person point of view. The central structure of an experience is its intentionality, its being directed toward something, as it is an experience of or about some object. An experience is directed toward an object by virtue of its content or meaning (which represents the object) together with appropriate enabling conditions."[94]

That melted my brain. Put simply, as a professional, the designer has an important opinion compared to other people. If you hire an interior designer to design your study, it is their artist's vision you hired not your own. The design should be true to that vision. If you do not like the design, then hire another designer, as all designers are different. This is the art component to design.

The field of design, particularly architecture, landscape and urban design all need to function as a building, landscape or city. A building needs to stand up. A city layout must not cause traffic jams, and plants in a landscape need to survive. This is the science component.

Today a revolution in design is coming and while in the middle of the COVID19 crisis, it is becoming more critical. We need evidence to back up our designs and we do not need random opinions. Our communities do not require artists, bold in their opinion but weak in their reasoning, designing our cities and landmarks.

This revolution comes in the form of Evidenced-Based Design (EBD). My first experience in EBD came while at an architectural company when they designed the Singapore Hospital. Doctors and nurses of the hospital had experienced a revolution in their industry in the form of Evidenced-Based Medicine, decades before. Both design and medical evidenced-based approaches have been around for a long time, but both fields of medicine and architecture had put the practitioner's experience ahead of all other knowledge. The head doctor was king; their opinion based on their experience, was the rule of law. After many litigation issues and the mounting evidence from researchers, over time, it was found the older doctor with all their experience was becoming out of touch with new and changing advancements. Their recommendations were questioned in the courtroom, and evidence was used like a revolutionary overthrowing the kings. Now a student doctor could override a seasoned doctor's opinion by showing evidence from the latest studies that proved differing opinions. Hospital rounds were changed into a discussion rather than a lecture from the head doctor. It became more democratic and less of a dictatorship, resulting in the best outcome for the patient.

When designing the hospital, doctors recognised this outdated behaviour in architects. The star architect would deliver the design and other architects would merely follow along. Doctors insisted that the design should not be a vision of one person but should be the result of using researched evidence that proved the design was best for the patient.

My company decided to build a full-scale hospital ward as a mock-up where patients, nurses and doctors could work for a few weeks, and all the data was collected and used to decide the best design outcomes for everyone, especially the patient.

Today this movement has spread into other areas of architecture, urban design, and town planning. Evidence is now required to explain why a street is designed as a curve. Is it because of the slope or to achieve more retail usage on the outside bend? We can no longer design a street only as an interesting experience for the driver.

Initially, EBD seems to be a very uncreative way of designing and relegates creativity to nothing more than pretty details on the periphery. The exact opposite is true. Many designers tend to use intuition when designing. They see places as comfortable and a feeling of naturalness about them. This intuition comes from life experience; it is all a learned and cultural subconscious feeling built up over the individual's lifetime. As a side note, this is why some people find homosexuality as abnormal. It is because they have not been exposed to it during their life. Gay people can easily hide within society, therefore to homophobic people, being gay feels unnatural to them. This led the gay rights movement to push people to 'come out', so everyone could see that gay people existed and to make it part of the cultural subconsciousness, the cultural norm.

The life experience, of exploring many places, people, and situations, gets replicated when a designer is designing new sites. Once designed, evidence-based research can step in to test if it works and most importantly, it can test *why* it works. This evidence gives weight to the scheme and helps to discard elements that do not function well.

An interesting example comes in art with paintings and also relates to the field of landscape architecture. There are many landscape paintings (and built parks) that show gently rolling hills of grass with trees planted wide apart, with a long view into the distance. I guarantee a park in your city, albeit, in Edinburgh, Osaka, Adelaide, Guangzhou or New York has a very similar park to this description. These places and the paintings feel natural to people, yet nature is a jungle in Guangzhou, a crowded forest of trees in Osaka and Edinburgh. Nature is a swamp in New York and a borderline desert in Adelaide. The earth has few natural landscapes that are like these parks with all examples being built by people. They are human-made landscapes and not made by nature. Humans made them as they are comfortable for us to be in. Yet there is one place on earth where this landscape did once naturally exist. It was in the Great Rift Valley in Ethiopia, one hundred thousand years ago.

This valley is where humans, through famine and predators, were reduced to a few thousand people and where all our ancestors come from today. It is the location where we are all evolved to live, our natural landscape. The broadly separated trees mean we had to walk from tree to tree rather than climb like monkeys, hence us evolving into walking rather than climbing beings. The views from the hilltops mean we could see predators coming, our eyes evolved for seeing at that distance. The lawns, which we pour billions of litres of water on to keep them alive and then cut them down with loud mowers, means two things. The grass height means animals are grazing nearby which are a source of food and the low height means predators can easily be seen, so the area feels safe. This theory is difficult to prove, and forms part of thoughts gathered by Evolutionary Psychological Theorists which explain elements of our designed world that no one else can.

Evidence-based design is a tool that helps us understand the processes going on in our constructed world or the need that drives us to climb one particular mountain over another. The Landmark Race is about gathering an understanding of landmarks that can provide us with evidence of what is successful about a landmark and what is mere folly. With all this in mind, a category in the landmark evaluation takes into account people's opinions, noting that the more opinions gathered, the more we receive a comprehensive understanding of what is popular, and we can look deeper into this to answer the big question of- *why*.

The Great Landmarks List

The Bucket Meta List of landmarks comes from the opinions formed by positive comments from TripAdvisor and by rankings mentioned at the beginning of this chapter by the various *opinion leaders*.

The landmarks that are added with no opinion component end up being lower in the list due to the fact they are less known. Sometimes it could be a result of poor marketing or little promotion. Yet, it also reflects the nuances of the architectural language that is required for comprehension not shared by the general public, as discussed in chapter 8. In the case of many notable landmarks in Iran or North Korea, they are not accessible to the rest of the world. We all live in this reality, and this is not a theoretical study. If

North Korea was capitalist and we could visit its landmarks weekly, it would rate higher. Accessibility is important, so is marketing, Instagram, and trends; these are elements that help a landmark's popularity. Therefore, if a landmark is not receiving online posts for any reasons, then the cause is still valid. If a landmark is not worth visiting because it is associated with an authoritarian regime, then that landmark is not that great, and its meaning is lessened.

Once a landmark is noticed, it takes an evidenced-based approach to sort them by greatness. That is where the other criteria discussed come into play and the great landmarks can be sorted and scored to reveal the greatest landmarks in the world.

10. The Score

"If I have seen further, it is by standing on the shoulders of Giants." Isaac Newton in 1675

There are many levels to look at and understand the world. A wine connoisseur may know the age of on oak barrel by merely tasting the wine. A geologist looking at a stone can comprehend the vast processes throughout its history to bring the rock to this location. An art expert can look at a painting and know what period, style and influences bought the artist to produce the piece. These are all a deeper understanding of the world around us and require a depth of language and knowledge to discern the greater meaning.

The more in-depth our knowledge of the world, the more complicated our world becomes. Even people who are considered a genius cannot do everything on their own. For example, one of the most common objects we have in our pocket, our mobile or cell phone, was not the invention of the founder of Apple, Steve Jobs. He did not wake up one day and put together an iPhone 7 in his garage. He was never that amazing that he could do it all on his own. There is also the famous genius, Leonardo da Vinci. He was a scientist, engineer, inventor, and artist. Yet if he were alive today, he would fail art school due to his poor Photoshop skills and his inability to turn on a computer. He could not be an engineer without at least knowing how to use a calculator and would have difficulties with doing complicated math. Leonardo's time in the 15th century was more straightforward than today, and it was easier to invent things when everything was yet to be invented. In the late 1400s, one man who had skills in drawing and representation, could communicate ideas and improve them over time, and be declared a genius.

Today, it takes hundreds of people to design a new version of a mobile phone, and even then, that version is based mostly on the previous version. The phone is an evolution of design and not a revolution. If we ask any one person in the world how the chip works for the central processor of that phone, no one person could answer without resorting to references and notes. How does the camera work? Not just notionally, sketch out how each circuit is laid out. Different people have access to various databases and documentation for each of the different specialisations. If any single person was put on an island to survive, could they even build a house before dying of hunger or thirst? As discussed in chapter 1 Isolation, we have all become specialists in narrow fields of a gigantic machine, and we need to come together to make it all work.

Buildings, too, are incredibly complicated. The brickwork must be laid evenly or the wall will fall. The foundations need to be a specific size to ensure the building does not collapse, and the soil needs to be analysed by an expert to determine its weight capacity. How is a nail made so it can hold two pieces of wood together? How is the metal mined to produce that nail? How is the drilling machine that mines the metal built? There is an infinite loop of a too-complex system that if we were to describe it to Leonardo da Vinci, he might drop out and become a house painter. The Mona Lisa painting would be nothing more than a flat square of eggshell white.

So, for discussion purposes, let's say there are two levels of understanding things in our world. One is at a deeper level. The language of architecture is on this level, so is art, landscape architecture, and engineering. Professionals in these fields need to be educated in all the detail. Some even specialise deeper into these fields, for example, residential housing design or civil road engineering. Many jobs today operate on this deeper level. Even coffee is subject to this with a broader range of everything from lattes to cold drip coffee, with a specialist coffee artist known as a barista trained to create your coffee masterpiece.

As the world becomes incredibly detailed, and our professions concern themselves with deeper, narrower levels of speciality, a new field is emerging that has boomed due to the availability of *big data*. This approach is the opposite in a way to the deep level approach we use as it looks across a wide spectrum. It concerns itself with generalisations rather than specifics. The best way of understanding this view of the world is to use the example of predicting the weather.

A few hundred years ago, the only way of knowing the weather was to go outside and look up. Clouds meant it might rain and the sun meant it was probably not going to rain. At this stage, predicting the weather was more of an art form and less of a science. It was more of a feeling than a result of evidence. Instruments like thermometers and barometers were developed to help measure the current weather, making predictions more accurate. It enabled us to see trends in the readings, to measure changes over time and through mathematical prediction, we were able to know with greater certainty that it might rain. Once we had devices located in many places, we could gather the data together and create a weather map to more accurately predict if it would rain. Today we have computer models that take all data, throughout time, and can foresee a seven-day forecast, show the long-term effects of global warming and predict longer-term droughts and floods. Meteorologists have modelled the whole planet and can experiment with changing future scenarios to see what outcomes can occur.

In the field of urban design, the Melbourne City Council predicts development trends by taking all the city's data throughout time and uses machine learning of the past to predict which parcels of land are likely to redevelop in the future. When all areas are combined, it decides what the population will be, how much retail space is needed and how much commercial space will be available in the future. Big data has allowed us to see into the future.

Big data is also used in marketing. Population trends can be examined to give specific details of individuals. In the past, the old way of doing marketing was like the tv show *Mad Men*. They used a creative team to create an advertisement they hoped people would respond to and buy the product. Now, with big data research, the market sectors are broken down, trends are followed, and predictions are made based on specific marketing approaches. An excellent example is when the retail store Target used its data to predict that a woman was pregnant based on her shopping habits and sent her brochures of baby carriages and formula before even the father knew. He found out by mail order.

The Landmarks List is a pulling together of data to create a *big data*-base. Less concerned with the details of a cornice of a building, the database takes a broad view of thousands of landmarks to pull out observations that only *big data* can reveal. Adding data from UNESCO World Heritage, its popularity, people's opinions, and its physical qualities show some of the surprising results discussed so far. For example, being the tallest does not automatically make a landmark great, and big does not matter so much unless there is a meaning behind it.

There was a lot more data added that were found to be useless in the Landmarks List. Its age alone was thought to be the only indicator of greatness. Yet, its cultural richness is more related to events and stories associated with the landmark and not just time. How it attracted the media was also thought to be an indicator of greatness and attractiveness; for example, the White House compared to the average house. This factor was difficult to measure, and the use of people's general opinion covered off this specific factor making it redundant. Another factor explored was the question: are there postcards of this landmark? It was found that there are postcards of everything, so this did not matter. A typology study was conducted; all landmarks were sorted into categories: mosques, cathedrals, temples, bridges etc., with analysis undertaken to see how it related to others in the category, as typical or atypical. Typology studies are common in urban design. It revealed nothing and ended up being far too subjective to derive anything more than my own opinion. Also, landmarks like the prison island of Alcatraz in San Francisco got lost in the typological study and ended up in a strange collection of landmarks called 'other'.

Tourism visitation numbers were also examined, but this was a consequence of the local population with a Chinese landmark always being the most popular and New Zealand landmarks being the most unpopular. International tourism numbers were also examined, but Europe as a place of many countries had far more international travellers than the United States, even though both had visitors that would have driven the same distance to a landmark. In the United States they would be considered local travellers and Europe they would be considered international.

Other categories of heritage, architectural greatness, natural beauty were all examined. Yet, it was found the UNESCO rating covered a lot of these factors without the variations from different countries.

The final list has over 370 landmarks with 2,000 landmarks cut due to low scores in the below categories:

- **Landmark**: As discussed in chapter 3, how much does it mark the land based on the dictionary definition.
- **Meaning**: The UNESCO World Heritage evaluation is used here with points given

based on how it meets the criteria discussed in chapter 7.
- **Memorable**: The research discussed in chapter 8 is used to give points by how memorable the landmark is based on its uses, shape and form.
- **Popularity**: This component is based on opinion leaders and positive online comments, as discussed in chapter 9.
- **Exceptional**: This category is rated less with only a couple of additional points added if the landmark is considered the tallest, or biggest, now or at some time in history. It is an indication of how a landmark can attract people's attention and visitors.

The highest possible score a landmark can achieve is 44.17; this is impossible. It would have to cover every UNESCO category, be a perfect landmark in definition, be both big and the tallest in the world, be the most memorable with many colours textures and stands alone with a complex shape. It would also be unanimously thought of as the greatest landmark in the world and have the highest amount of positive online comments. The lowest possible score is zero. An underground cave of no natural or cultural significance would achieve this score.

11. The Results

The top ten greatest landmarks are:

1. Eiffel Tower in Paris, France (26.69)
2. Sagrada Familia in Barcelona, Spain (24.47)
3. Colosseum in Rome, Italy (24.28)
4. Taj Mahal in Agra, India (23.30)
5. Acropolis in Athens, Greece (22.73)
6. Hagia Sophia in Istanbul, Turkey (22.39)
7. Cathedral Santa Maria di Fiore in Florence, Italy (21.61)
8. Machu Picchu in Cusco, Peru (21.56)
9. Pyramid of Giza in El Gizeh, Egypt (21.48)
10. St Basil's Cathedral in Moscow, Russia (21.46)

The final list is a result of the previous analysis with a valid reason why each landmark is ranked higher than another. Yet, I feel the Pyramid of Giza at number nine should be higher. It was pointed out to me that there are two pyramids on either side of the Pyramid of Giza, and this makes it less unique, and there are also many pyramids in the Nile Valley and both South and Central America. It also scores lower than the others because of its lack of uses – it is just a tomb, its *use singularity* (use compared to the other uses around it) is also low, as the Nile Valley has many tombs and pyramids. Therefore, I had to concede that the Pyramids of Giza are not the greatest landmark in the world. When I visited this landmark, I went inside to the burial chamber at its core. The tunnel roof is just over a metre high, and I had to crouch to walk down. There were only a few people in the tunnel at the time due to the political instability in Egypt, yet there was still little oxygen. I had to take multiple breaths to stop myself from suffocating. My experience of this landmark was the most powerful experience of a landmark I have had. It has a remarkable history, yet I do concede it is not as unique as the others and I must put my bias aside.

The Sagrada Familia at number two is incredibly unusual as a landmark. It is still under construction, yet it is UNESCO Heritage protected; there is no building like this in the list. The Colosseum is two thousand years old and still stands like it is waiting for a football game in the centre of modern Rome, that is remarkable.

Europe is well represented in the Landmarks List with 182 entries of the shortened list, well over double Asia as the next continent with only 89. The reason for this is twofold. In Europe, the Christian religion is dominated by cathedrals with a tradition of constructing buildings to last. The builders felt that the buildings should reflect god and be solid and eternal. Therefore, the structures were always over-engineered and predominantly built of stone. Secondly, the approach to heritage in Europe is to maintain the buildings in their original form with the original materials, bricks, beams, etc., all of their original construction. A building is the sum of its parts and it should be authentic. They are maintained in their original form. While in Asia, a lot of their landmarks are constructed of wood, particularly in Japan. As the wood ages and warps over time, the beams are replaced. Effectively the building is totally replaced.

The differences in global heritage protection approaches can be experienced in Seam Reap, Cambodia. The Bayon Temple at Angkor is the 19th greatest landmark. During a tour of the site, the guide pointed out to me that a Chinese contingency restored the temple of Chau Say Tevoda and their approach was to locate the fallen stonework and position them in their original locations. If stones were missing, new stones were made and put in place. Whereas other temples restored by French or German contingents had put back the stones they knew to be correct and left on the ground those whose location was uncertain. The temples in Seam Reap are famous for the jungle regrowing amongst the ruins. Some trees have grown from between the stonework, pushing them apart and stretching over the ruins. Some of the

European restorations kept these trees as features. They only controlled the damage caused by the jungle, differing from the Chinese approach of removing all vegetation and turning the ground into a lawn.

Paris Landmarks

In a weekend trip to Paris, you can see eight of the world's greatest landmarks but do not get overly distracted by artwork inside the Louvre, at number 22, which pushes up this landmark in the opinion category. The building itself as a landmark is less remarkable in the Paris context. Still, the glass pyramid entry, on direct alignment along the Champs Elysees to the Arc de Triumph (74th), is remarkable. If you head directly south from the Arc de Triumph, across the River Seine, you will arrive at the greatest landmark in the world, the Eiffel Tower.

The tower is a purpose-built flagship attraction, as it functions mostly as a landmark and as a tourist attraction with a viewing deck. It loses points for its lack of uses or functions, but every other aspect, including its UNESCO status, boost it to the top. It was initially a temporary structure that was disliked during construction, yet it is so popular today and will last an eternity.

Next landmark on this tour is Notre Dame de Paris, the cathedral was built between 1163 and 1345, and ranks at 18th in the world. It suffered fire damage in 2019, which was worse than the damage caused during the

French Revolution between 1787 to 1799. It was ransacked with many of the statues destroyed to make bullets.

Another church worth a visit is the Basilique du Sacre-Coeur de Montmartre ranked at number 105. It is located on top of a hill with the Moulin Rouge, number 187th, located near the bottom of the same hill. Finally, the Pompidou Centre, built in the 1960s is at number 236 and the Musée d'Orsay, a former Beaux-Arts railway station now housing impressionist masterpieces is 180th in the world.

Most Landmarks

The United Kingdom has the most top-rated landmarks in the world, with 35, and the United States comes in second with 30 landmarks. London has 14 of these top landmarks. Big Ben comes in at number 20. In this sense Big Ben refers to the clock tower, renamed Elizabeth Tower in 2012, and part of to the British Houses of Parliament, 127th greatest. Officially Big Ben is the name of the bell inside the clock on the north side of the tower, yet many people misname it. The clock tower is 96 metres tall and situated on the north bank of the River Thames. Hidden from the river, behind the Houses of Parliament, is Westminster Abbey, the 104th greatest landmark, which is over a thousand years old.

On the south bank, just downstream and across from Big Ben, is the 50th greatest landmark in the world, the

London Eye. It was built as a temporary Ferris wheel for the millennium, yet it has become a permanent feature of the city. The Tate Modern art museum (140th) is further down on the southern bank with St Paul's Cathedral (165th) opposite on the north bank. The Tower of London (129th) completes our river journey. Behind this bank is the recently constructed Shard office tower(146th) with the previously known Swiss Re Building, 20 St Mary Axe, also known as The Gherkin due to its shape. This office building is 149th in the world. Finally, there is the Natural History Museum at 255, the British Museum at 273, Buckingham Palace at 255 and Piccadilly Circus, which incorporates the plaza space and surrounding buildings at number 336, all located around central London.

The rest of the United Kingdom has 21 of the world's greatest landmarks consisting of chapels, abbeys, and castles. Two outstanding landmarks of note are Stonehenge, an ancient series of stones arranged in a circle which is over 4,000 years old (113th), and the Eden Project, only 20 years old. The Eden Project incorporates a series of circular biodomes as protected gardens from around the world, and comes in at number 231.

Religion

Religion dominates the list of greatest landmarks with 84 of the 368 landmarks in the world associated with it. These all come under the typologies of either a church, cathedral, temple, shrine, monastery, or mosque. The cathedral Sagrada Familia, in Barcelona, is the second greatest landmark in the world and highlights the importance of religious institutions to present themselves as a landmark in our cities and towns. Historically, as explained in the Race for Tall chapter, religious buildings were developed to represent god and their presence, towering over a village was a constant reminder to the people that god was ever-present.

Many religious buildings are under UNESCO Heritage protection and due to their importance and frequency of visitors, attract historical events. All the Kings and Queens of England have had their coronations in Westminster Abbey. King Henry III was crowned in Gloucester (in 1216), due to rebels having control of London, he opted for a second coronation in Westminster Abbey once the rebels were defeated.

The highest-ranked Mosque is at number 6, the Hagia Sophia in Turkey. Constructed initially as a Christian basilica around 1,500 years ago it suffered a fire in 532 and was rebuilt. To rebuild it to be a great landmark that representative of all the Byzantine Empire, Emperor Justinian demanded all provinces under his rule to send architectural pieces for use in its construction.

"The marble used for the floor and ceiling was produced in Anatolia (present-day eastern Turkey) and Syria, while other bricks (used in the walls and parts of

the floor) came from as far away as North Africa. The interior of Hagia Sophia is lined with enormous marble slabs that are said to have been designed to imitate moving water. And, the Hagia Sophia's 104 columns were imported from the Temple of Artemis in Ephesus, as well as from Egypt."[95]

Once the Republic of Turkey was established in 1935, the landmark operated as a museum and attracted more than three million visitors a year. However, Islamic religious leaders have pressured the government to convert the landmark back to a mosque.

If we travel further east to Myanmar, we will find the world's greatest temple at number 16, the Shwedagon Pagoda. A circular building with the same silhouette as the Eifel tower but spun around on a potter's wheel. It is constructed of bricks covered in gold plate. The top is covered in 5,448 diamonds and 2,317 rubies with the very tip being said to hold a 76-carat diamond. There are four entrances to the temple at each compass point with guard statues known as Chinthes at the openings to the compound. The pagoda is the most sacred site for Buddhists in Myanmar. It has stood in the city of Rangoon, at the height of 112 metres, for over 650 years. (See Figure 31.)

Figure 31: Shwedagon Pagoda, Myanmar.

The construction of religious landmarks has waned over the last few decades with the rise of mega-churches; religious organisations that operate more like a corporation than a church. The new religious landmarks look more like stadiums and concert arenas than they do religious landmarks. There are two exceptions to this in the list. The first is the Metropolitan Cathedral of Brasília ranked at 141 and the Lotus Temple in New Delhi, India, ranked at 132.

The Cathedral in Brasilia was built from 1958 to 1970 with a capacity of over four thousand people. It is a Roman Catholic church shaped like a modernist crown with large white, boomerang-shaped supports all leaning against each other to form a circle. The roof between the supports is constructed of coloured glass shaped in ribbons of light and dark with blue banding around it. (See Figure 32: Cathedral of Brasília.)

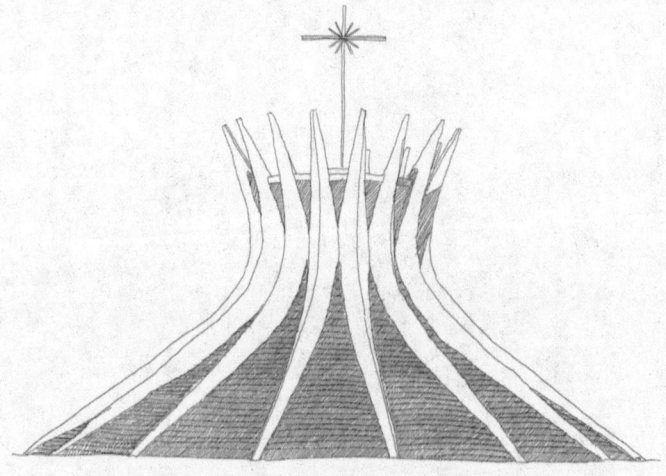

Figure 32: Cathedral of Brasília

The Lotus Temple was built in 1986 and is also circular as if someone took the white sails from the Sydney Opera house and arranged them to all lean on each other around a central axis. More accurately, it intentionally looks like a lotus flower. The temple is open to all religions and can accommodate 2,500 people. It has won many architectural awards and has been visited by over 100 million tourists since its opening in 1986 to 2014. (See Figure 33.)

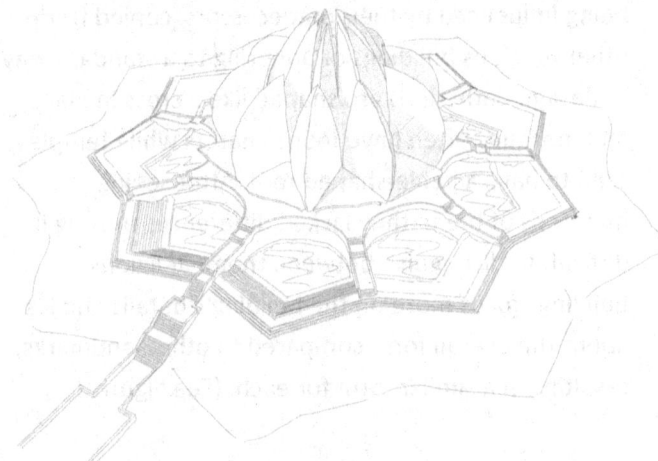

Figure 33: Lotus Temple, India.

The most unusual entry is at number 296. It is the Temppeliaukio Church in Helsinki, Finland. It appears from the street as a dome surrounded by a pile of rocks in a medium-rise suburban neighbourhood. It is located partially underground, hence its poor score as a landmark. It is built into solid rock with a ring of windows supporting the circular dome. It was built in 1969 for the Lutheran church and can hold 750 people for worship and gives the feeling of being part of the earth rather than of heaven like most religious building strive to achieve.

In processing the list of landmarks, churches, mosques, and temples dominate the list due to their UNESCO Heritage, religious popularity and their prominence as a landmark to attract attention and worshippers. After a lengthy review, few stood out as unusual, with many being influenced by their predecessors, copied from other religious buildings or adhering to a standard way of design. Cathedrals are shaped like a cross in plan, and mosques often have four minarets while temples tend to have a gable-shaped roof. After seeing hundreds of them, they lacked differences making it difficult to distinguish between them. Religious buildings focus more on the building's details and less about the overall form compared to other landmarks, resulting in a similar form for each. (See Figure 34.)

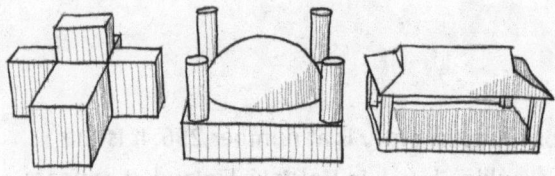

Figure 34: From left to right, standard forms of churches, mosques, and temples.

Bridges

Bridges make for great landmarks for a few reasons.

1. Mostly they are prominent. Often crossing a waterbody, and open to views in both directions and if large ocean liners are to travel underneath it, their height can be seen for miles around.
2. They are a significant point for activity. They funnel the city's traffic down to a single

    crossing point creating a hive of movement back and forth.
3. Bridges take engineering expertise to span large distances giving them an unusual, recognisable shape.
4. Their function is enhanced by contrast to the buildings on their banks. They differ significantly in function and shape.

The only way to avoid a bridge being a landmark is to build a tunnel. Tunnels are standard practice in many cities that already have a great landmark bridge. The reason for building tunnels is to avoid distraction from another landmark bridge. The Sydney Harbour Bridge is an excellent example of this.

Spanning between the Sydney CBD and the North Shore, the Sydney Harbour Bridge was the widest bridge in the world until 2012 when it lost the title to the wider Port Mann Bridge in Vancouver.

The Harbour Bridge was built in 1932. My grandmother attended the opening, my father held in her arms as a baby. There were 750,000 people at the event and just as the ribbon was to be cut by the officials, Francis De Groot, a member of the ultra-right-wing New Guard group, rode out of the crowd on horseback and slashed the ribbon with his cavalry sword. The officials tied the ribbon back together, and the Premier cut it again with Francis receiving a fine of five pounds[96]. My father told me this story and how my grandmother then walked across the crowded bridge, only finding space on the railway tracks. She stepped from sleeper to sleeper, avoiding the large gaps with the water 50 metres below, my father still in her arms.

The bridge has stood since that day as a great world icon. Its four pylons – two on either bank – are built for aesthetic purposes to visual bookend the bridge, creating its iconic shape. One of the pylons was later utilised as an exhaust vent for the Harbour Tunnel. When traffic on the bridge required another, city planners knew they could not compete with its iconic status, so rather than build a competing bridge, a tunnel was the best solution. It seems fair that the bridge should have an exhaust vent in it, considering it gets to retain its splendour as the only bridge crossing the harbour. (See Figure 8: Sydney Harbour Bridge.)

The bridge design was chosen in an international design competition with Dorman Long & Co Ltd being the winner. The steel company also submitted alternative designs; for example, a bridge with three smaller arches, and a reverse design with each end larger and the centre smaller. There was a design in an alternate location on the harbour, intersecting Goat Island with a tower and war memorial spanning the bridge in three directions[97]. There was a simple flat design with no upper structure and a design that looked like the Golden Gate Bridge.

The Golden Gate Bridge in San Francisco is the greatest landmark bridge in the world. It is also the greatest landmark in the United States, at number 11, and is ranked just above the Statue of Liberty. The reason for this is its usefulness at crossing over to the city from Marin County, and its frequency of activity gives it a slight boost, not to mention its distinctive red colour. It is in more lists of greatest landmarks than Lady Liberty and has nearly 10,000 more positive comments on TripAdvisor yet does not have the UNESCO Heritage status the statue enjoys. It has been noted as one of the modern wonders of the world by the American Society of Engineers, lifting its fame. Its massive size gives it an edge as a landmark.

The Rialto Bridge in Venice, Italy, is the second bridge in the list ranked at number 23. The bridge vastly differs in size being only 7.3 metres in height compared to the Golden Gate Bridge's 67 metres. (See Figure 35.) The Rialto Bridge spans the Grand Canal and if we cut a section through it, we see:

- A walkway on the water's edge
- a row of shops facing the centre
- the central stepped walkway
- another row of shops facing in
- another waterside walkway on the other side.

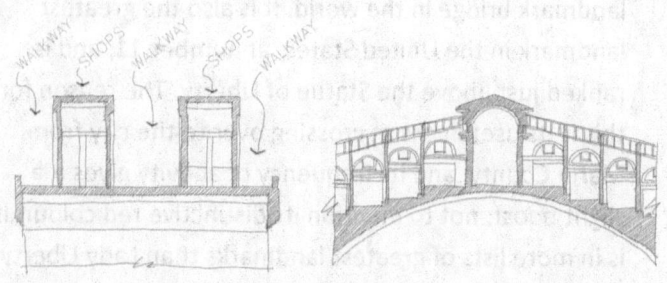

Figure 35: Rialto Bridge Cross section.

Souvenir stores now dominate the rows of shops. The idea of placing shops on a bridge is brilliant and I wonder why more bridges do not do this. Bridges act as a funnel point for traffic, forcing all people to pass the shopping outlets. The Rialto Bridge was built 430 years ago replacing a floating pontoon bridge that dates from 1173. I wonder if the more recent separation of engineering from architecture has caused our bridges today to be so single functioned.

The Rialto Bridge is not the oldest in the list, Pont Du Gard in France is, ranked at number 66 and dates back to the year 60. It has UNESCO Heritage status and was built by the Romans to transport water across the Gardon River as an aqueduct. Its length is 275 metres, and it stands at the height of 48.8 metres. The Romans built a series of arches with the bottom two rows being large and the top rows being a series of smaller arches. From today's standpoint, it is quite unusual that for a large structure to be used for water to cross water. A sealed enclosed pipe could run down the banks and back up with ease, making the bridge construction redundant. Romans did not have the technology to make a leak-proof pipe, so they resorted to grand aqueducts and creating impressive landmarks.

The Millau Viaduct, also in France, ranks at number 84 and it is the opposite to the Pont Du Gard. It is a modern bridge built in 2004 crossing the Gorge Valley. It is a recently built great landmark standing at over 330 metres high. It appears like a series of bridges; all held up by cables linked together in a chain. As the world's tallest bridge, it also stretches for just under two and a half kilometres. It appears as if someone has drawn a line through the sky above the quaint French countryside. (See figure 36.)

Figure 36: The Millau Viaduct, France.

The smallest bridge in the list is the Japanese Covered Bridge in Hoi An, Vietnam. The town existed as a trading port on the Thu Bon River delta, just before it opens out to sea. It operated as a trading port and is prone to flooding. When I was working on a project in the area, a shop owner showed me how the town deals with flooding. The shops all have a sparse ground floor with living and storage all located on the upper floors. When the water begins to rise, shop keepers use a series of ropes and pulleys, to hoist the furniture up to the second floor through trap doors, leaving the ground level to flood. The Japanese Covered Bridge is in the centre of this town and crosses a small canal. It is ranked 213th in the list. It was opened in 1719 and built by the local Japanese community to reach the Chinese quarter. The bridge features sculptures of dogs and monkeys representing the Chinese calendar years in which it was constructed. The cultural motifs on this bridge are representative of the mix of people that frequented the trading port. The design includes Vietnamese, Japanese and Chinese elements.

Most bridges are designed to cross waterways with little interruption of the flow, yet Iran has an unusual bridge crossing the Zayanderud River, that does the opposite. Built in 1650, the Khaju Bridge acts as a dam, allowing pedestrians to cross at the spillway. The bridge has two arched colonnades, one on top of the other, with a hexagonal pavilion at the centre. Water is held back on one side and passes through a series of slots to create small waterfalls on the other. The bridge is ranked at number 320, and it is not protected under UNESCO World Heritage. There are only around 1000 positive comments on TripAdvisor for this landmark and it is only mentioned on one list of great landmarks, hence its poor score.

Some other bridges in the list are the Brooklyn Bridge in New York City at number 28, the Charles Bridge in Prague at number 39, and Ponte Vecchio in Florence at number 53.

Nature

Mother nature can make a great landmark too. The tallest landmark in the world is Mount Everest, ranked at 264. A mountain is a typical example of a natural landmark, yet they are also part of human culture with the human desire to climb and 'conquer' it. The notion that a mountain is conquered by climbing it is a strange idea and is part of a primitive human urge.

When a person looks up to a mountain, it is unknown, and it never fully understood until it is climbed. People standing at its summit can see all around them. Some liken it to being close to god. Numerous mountain temples use this feeling and utilise this natural human instinct of wishing to be in a high location.

When archaeologists analysed primitive Homo sapien campsites in Europe their locations would often be on the top of hills. Archaeologists noted that it always made sense to them to locate the camp areas in these locations as it provides a view up and down the valley. Alternatively, when they examined Neanderthals campsites, they were found to be in unusual places, often near water and on lower land. Neanderthals are a different species to humans (Homo sapiens), and their sense of where to camp was alien to the archaeologists. Yet, the Homo sapiens, our ancestors, felt perfectly reasoned and understandable. We all have a deep instinct to be in high places, places with a view – the greater the view, the greater the place. This also helps us understand why many great landmarks, including the Eiffel tower, have viewing decks and why mountains are so important to us.

The greatest natural landmark in the world is Cradle Mountain in the Tasmanian Wilderness, the 25th greatest landmark in the world. You would be excused for not knowing this landmark. Its popularity rating holds it back, only having 1000 positive comments on TripAdvisor. Yet its UNESCO World Heritage status, of meeting seven of the ten categories, pulls it towards the top. It is a natural feature with unique plant and animal life known only to this location, and it has cultural importance in the form of Aboriginal Cultural Heritage. Aborigines in Tasmania experienced genocide at the hands of the first European settlers making this area even more important to the descendants, and as a historical record for all the world.

Also, in Australia and next at number 26, is Uluru in the Northern Territory. This gigantic single rock feature measuring 20 metres taller than the Eiffel Tower stands out amongst the flat outback desert. Its perimeter is 9.4 kilometres and its bright red sandstone colour is nothing less than impressive during sunrise and sunset, as it changes colour with the changing light. It ticks only four UNESCO boxes, but its popularity pushes it up the list. To the culturally unaware, Uluru beckons people to climb and conquer it, yet it is a sacred site to the local Aṉangu community who request visitors not to climb the rock. Many visitors do, however. With signs informing them of the significance, they still feel it is okay to add to the worn trail in the soft sandstone and climb its western face. I wonder how these climbers would feel if an Aboriginal person climbed up an ancient cathedral, brushing gargoyles and angels on their way up? On the 26th of October 2019, a ban came into effect that prevents visitors from climbing the landmark and the chains bolted into the rock face were removed.

The desire to climb has had the opposite effect on other natural features through the construction of grand complexes at their peaks. Ranked as the 5th greatest landmark in the world is the Acropolis of Athens. Dating from 500 BCE, the mountain complex's main feature is the Parthenon, an ancient Roman temple to the goddess Athena. The 8th greatest landmark is Machu Picchu in Peru which was a village located on a prominent mountain ridge. Constructed around 1450 AD but abandoned a century later, many of the ruins have been restored to give tourists a better idea of its original form.

Victoria Peak Tower in Hong Kong (200th) is an example of a more active tourist attraction. It has the Peak Tower, an upside-down semicircular building with a viewing deck on its flat upper side. The building houses souvenir shops and restaurants. Its unusual shape is recognisable from across the harbour. The building also houses a tram terminus with trams that climb up the steep mountain. The tram is on a permanent angle with the corridor constructed with steps and the seats all bend up to be vertical.

The Rock of Gibraltar (222nd) is a 426-metre-high limestone monolith that stands at the entrance to the Mediterranean Sea. The upper area is a nature reserve that has the only wild monkeys in Europe. The mountain has a series of tunnels constructed over 200 years for storage and artillery use by the British army. The rock's prominent position at the sea entrance and its height put it in an incredibly strategic position during war and its ownership by the British, surrounded by Spain, is retained for that purpose.

Two mountains worthy of mentioning due to their unusual shape is Table Mountain (158th), in Cape Town and Mount Roraima in Venezuela (279th). Both mountains have a flat, square top to them. Table Mountain is surrounded by the city of Cape Town making the landmark more active with cable car access, yet Mount Roraima is more exact in shape with a flat top and sheer cliffs dropping down to the valley. It looks abstract and unnatural, like excavators constructed it.

Mount Eden Crater is also an interesting natural landmark as it sits surrounded by the city of Auckland in New Zealand and is a mountain with a large depression in the centre. So smooth with its lawn, it seems like it is carved by an artist.

Waterbodies appear in the Great Landmarks List, although they make for poor landmarks. Moraine Lake, at 360, in Banff National Park Canada, is a bright turquoise lake surrounded by steep mountains. It is fed by Fay Glacier and Larch Creek and is only 14 metres deep, yet it is half a square kilometre in size. It is not considered a landmark due to its size and that the surrounding mountains dominate it. It is not UNESCO Heritage protected and rates lower on the opinion ratings. Lakes tend to lack the activity a greater landmark has.

The higher-rated waterbodies tend to be thermal baths. Széchenyi Thermal Baths in Budapest ranks second highest for waterbodies, at number 233. Opened in 1913 the baths are fed by a naturally heated spring, one at 74 °C (165 °F), and the other at 77 °C (171 °F) but the baths are constructed as a series of swimming pools. The surrounding building adds to the visual quality of these pools as a landmark and the presence of swimmers add activity raising its rating.

The highest-rated water body is not natural at all. It is the Trevi Fountain in Rome at number 49. Built in 1762 and bundled in with the UNESCO Heritage protection for central Rome. It incorporates the vertical façade of a neighbouring building in its form, creating a landmark that is more visible from a distance, boosting it higher in its ranking.

If water is to be considered a landmark then in needs to fall. Waterfalls are the most common water bodies in the Great Landmarks List. Victoria Falls (138th) in Zimbabwe is the largest in terms of single width, at 1.7 kilometres, and ranked at 262 is Iguazu Falls in Brazil which has a total combined width of 2.7 kilometres. Both regard themselves as the largest in the world. Niagara Falls on the Canadian and United States border tends to be the most popular and the most visited waterfall, ranked at number 278.

A very unusual natural feature due to its curiously shaped stones is the Giant's Causeway in Northern Ireland ranked at number 287. Located on the north coast at the edge of the sea are a series of 40,000 interlocking, seven or eight-sided basalt columns that rise out of the water. They look like they were perfectly manufactured, like hexagonal paving, but they extrude in places to create columns. They were formed naturally as the lava cooled 50-60 million years ago, in a similar way as mud will dry on a hot summer's day.

Old and New

To be a great landmark it can pay to be old, although it is not guaranteed. Age brings with its acceptance from the local community for those landmarks considered too radical. Age can also bring it cultural depth in the form of stories and events associated with it over its lifetime. Yet there is no formula for age. I attempted to create a formula in the rating system but it was too inconsistent as cultural depth does not equal age and relates more to the meanings associated with it rather than the number of years it has been around.

The highest-ranked and also youngest landmark in the list (depending on how high and how young we look) is the Golden Gate Bridge at number 11, built-in 1937. Next would be the Sydney Opera House at number 21, built-in 1973, followed by the Burj Al Arab in Dubai at number 38. This building is a five-star hotel that sits on a small artificial island connected to the mainland and stands at thirty storeys in height. It has the appearance of a boat sail with a bend on one side. It was built in 1994. The next youngest is the London Eye Ferris wheel built in 2000 at number 50. The tallest building in the world, the Burj Khalifa comes in next at number 62, built-in 2009.

To become a great landmark and be relatively new, takes an engineering or design feat to make the landmark unique. Being the tallest in the world can achieve this when constructed, but as time moves on and another landmark takes the record, the building will drop down the list into obscurity.

The oldest landmarks in the list are, of course, natural landmarks as they were formed before human existence. The Pyramid of Giza is the oldest and one of the greatest human-made landmarks ranked at number nine, although the Colosseum, aged just under 2000 years old, is also in the race, and is ranked higher at number three.

The Odd

The Sagrada Familia ranked as the second greatest landmark, is both old and new. Its construction began in 1882 and is aiming to be complete in 2026. It is designed by one man but adapted and designed by many others over its one hundred years of construction. It is UNESCO Heritage protected, yet unlike other protected landmarks, it is not being preserved and is still being modified. It is also extremely popular and visited by millions. Like the Eiffel Tower, it was odd when it was built but has grown into acceptance as construction has progressed.

The aim of this analysis in finding the greatest landmark is also to find what qualities make a landmark great. Being odd, or unique, is both very satisfying and an unsatisfying answer as this cannot be quantified. For a landmark to be great, it must not be like anything else, in one or more aspects of its shape or meaning. It may be messy, like the Sagrada Familia, neat like the Eiffel Tower, simple as a pyramid or complex as Mont Saint Michel or tall like the Burj Khalifa, or long like the Golden Gate Bridge. Oddness seems to be the main predominant factor that all great landmarks have in common. If there was a way of measuring oddness and designing to an odd scale, we would have a world filled with great landmarks, one on every block. The only way of determining oddness is to know what has been done before and to do something different. Therefore, it takes knowledge of all the world's greatest landmarks to invent something unique.

12. Winning the Race

To be a great landmark, it needs to be odd or unique in some way. Uniqueness may take the form of a fascinating historical story, shape, or in its accolades as being the tallest, widest, or biggest. In reviewing the world's most significant landmarks, it also seems that the more qualities of uniqueness a landmark has, the greater it is.

If we design a building that is shaped like a rounded upside-down cup and placed it in London, it may be confused with the Gherkin Building (30 St Mary Axe), or the dome of Saint Pauls Cathedral. Yet, if the building was placed in outback Australia, on a flat desert plain, it would stand out as a more spectacular landmark. However, to be the greatest in the whole world, it needs to be unique in the context of the entire world. Effectively it needs to compete with everything around it as well as with all other landmarks in the world in uniqueness, to make it the greatest.

Uniqueness is not measurable in any objective sense; we cannot give a score for how unique a landmark is, as we need to compare that landmark to all others, to assess how it differs. Yet the Great Landmarks List does have a series of measurable correlations which approximate uniqueness and if designers follow this, it can help in creating more great world icons.

Accessibility

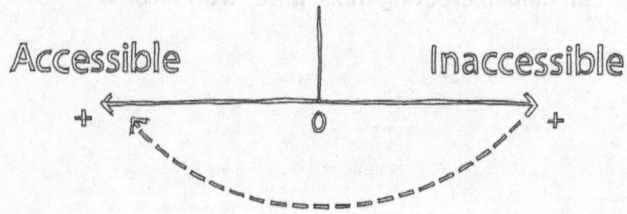

Figure 37: Accessibility

Landmarks fall into a spectrum between being highly accessible (easy to get to) and highly inaccessible (difficult to get to). A central city landmark has a high degree of accessibility. They are close to hotels and public transport. Locals can even visit it in their lunch hour. I worked a street away from St Pauls in London and would take a tour every few months. The more accessible a landmark is, the more popular the landmark can become. Inversely, landmarks can also be inaccessible. Mont Saint Michel, 13th greatest landmark is built on a rocky hill on an island and is incredibly inaccessible. Neuschwanstein Castle (15th) is on a rocky hilltop, the Statue of Liberty is on an island and Christ the Redeemer is on a mountain peak. The inaccessibility makes these landmarks unique. The area in-between on the spectrum, if the landmark is just inconvenient to get to then this lessens the greatness of that landmark. A useful example of being in the middle of the accessibility spectrum is a landmark located in a city suburb. It requires someone to drive to it, but it is easy to enter, this lessens the overall experience of the landmark. Most of the top landmarks are highly accessible, or they are unique due to their inaccessibility. A mountain top temple built around a rocky outcrop is great because of its location, yet a temple next to the highway is not so great.

Inaccessibility does not mean that a visitor cannot get there. In many cases, a creative form of transport is required to see that landmark thus enhancing the experience. The Statue of Liberty requires a ferry ride, the Peak in Hong Kong has the sloping tram, cable cars are used for many mountain-based landmarks, or hundreds of steps are needed to reach some temples. This creation of a specialised transport mode to experience an inaccessible landmark gives the landmark the advantage of capitalising on its inaccessibility but still makes it easy to visit. Figure 37: Accessibility, shows the more accessible or inaccessible a landmark is, the greater the landmark. Yet if a creative form of transport is used, it can benefit from both the advantages of being inaccessible and the advantages being accessible.

Location

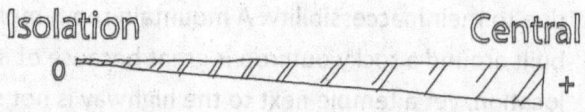

Figure 38: International Location

Location is not the same as accessibility and needs to be thought of on an international scale. How remote or central a landmark's location (not the landmark itself) can be influenced by global politics, airport locations, trains, flight availability, safety, currency exchange rates and entrance fee prices. With international sanctions and safety concerns for visitors, Naqsh-e Jahan Square in Iran is difficult for many people in the world to visit. Yet, its other qualities boost it to 125th greatest landmark in the world. Its location hinders it from being higher. The Mansudae Grand Monument in Pyongyang, North Korea, also suffers from a similar fate. Uluru in Outback Australia, on the other hand, is in one of the safest countries in the world to travel, it is boosted higher due to a dedicated airport and frequent commercial flights and local hotels, even though it is in one of the remotest locations in the world. Location is a contributing factor affecting the greatness of landmarks and comes into consideration when we think about how great they are. If we wish our landmarks to be great, then transport infrastructure, accommodation or even a political change may be required to move it up the rank. (See Figure 38: International Location.)

Style, form, and shape.

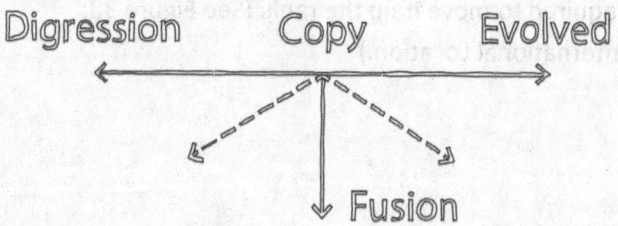

Figure 39: Style, form, and shape. Right is considered great and left is considered inferior

Purposefully this book does not discuss architectural style. As discussed earlier, architectural style forms part of an architectural language that is best understood through the range of literature available on the topic. The focus here is on an understanding of architecture from those not fluent in the language. Looking at a simple reading of a building, typical to the way a mass tourist would understand it, is more valuable. In this sense, style can be considered in a similar way to form and shape. All three aspects are critical components to creating a great landmark.

The greatest landmarks are not just an excellent example of a particular style; they also have to be better than what has gone before it. A typical example are the cathedrals of Europe. These buildings all utilise the knowledge of churches built before them and are constructed to a similar style and shape, yet the great ones improve on this and enhance it. A landmark that simply copies a style, form, or shape from another landmark is less than the original. If the copy is worse, it can be considered a digression. The more advanced or evolved a landmark is, the higher its rating. The Bayon Temple at Angkor Wat is an example of an evolved style, form, and shape, as it utilises building traditions yet enhances it so much that it gets considered as a new style.

Great landmarks are those that are evolved from previous styles into a new style. They are not revolutionary styles plucked out of thin air. As with most things in our world, extreme styles have been tried. For example, Sharp Centre for Design, OCAD University in Canada is a gigantic box-shaped building with black and white squares floating above buildings in the street supported by leaning coloured columns. The Royal Ontario Museum, also in Canada, is also a revolutionary example and both are difficult to describe as we lack a common language to describe it. The lack of language is what holds back revolutionary design. We communicate, think, and learn using language. If we do not have the language to understand a landmark, then it remains lost to us. Therefore, sometimes great architecture, to architects, are known to have evolved from other designs. Yet, to everyone else it is revolutionary, and they will not have the words to understand it. These buildings get hated.

Furthermore, landmarks can be designed with the fusion of different styles. It is typical for a post-modernist building to be designed in this way. An example of a fusion of styles is the Sagrada Familia with its combination of Gothic and curvilinear Art Nouveau forms. However, the design for the Cathedral is an evolution of both these styles. It is a mix of improved styles all adding up to it being one of the greatest landmarks in the world.

The Eiffel Tower was hated and thought revolutionary when it was built, but in time people learnt that it was an evolved version of a tower with that of railway bridge design. The styles were merged and not as revolutionary as first thought. Once this is understood, acceptance follows.

If the landmark gets copied, like the many Eiffel Tower copies, into a lesser version of the style (a digression), then it is considered inferior. (See Figure 39.)

Time

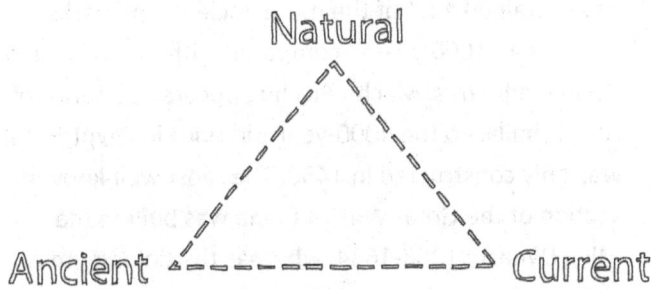

Figure 40: Natural landmarks are an exception to the rule of time

We value older landmarks. Yet, the older things are, the more lost they become to our understanding of them. The pyramids remain a mystery to many people, although their construction is not a real mystery with a lot of evidence proving how they were built. An ancient pile of stones can be considered virtually sacred if old enough, but if they were piled up by your friend on their beach vacation, no one would care. Put simply the older, the better. This factor differs when we take into consideration natural landmarks. Natural features are the oldest landmarks (except for some volcanos), yet humans regard them as less important. It is an anthropocentric understanding of the world that humans are the most crucial factor when it comes to landmarks, even at the detriment of our natural world and environment.

Time has differing levels of value for human-made landmarks around the world. Europe and North Africa have retained a lot of the more ancient landmarks (older than 1000 years), compared with American and Asian landmarks. Machu Picchu appears as a series of ruins, similar to the 4000-year-old ruins in Egypt, yet it was only constructed in 1450. The most well-known section of the Great Wall of China was built in the Ming Dynasty 1368-1644, whereas the Colosseum is still standing in the City of Rome like a new football stadium 2000 years after it was constructed.

(Figure 40 shows the three-way spectrum of age.)
Age is not strictly the older, the better. Landmarks that have a suite of historical events associated with it and have significant meaning attached to them rise higher in the ranking than those that are ancient.

Big

Figure 41: Big is better.

An undeniable trait that comes out as significant in the data is that they tend to be big. In comparing many of the landmarks, it was evident that if a landmark can be made bigger than its predecessor, then it can supersede it. In the chapter, The Race for Tall, the need for great landmarks to be tall, is discussed. It follows a common human trait and all civilisations tend to value this. It is also true for the creation of big roadside attractions in the form of the Big Pineapple, Banana or Orange. Yet it is the addition of meaning to this size that can make a landmark genuinely great. The Golden Gate Bridge needs to be big to span the great distance between the two peninsulas. The Great Wall of China needs to be long to act as a barrier. The Eiffel Tower needs to be tall to create the most incredible views, and the Statue of Liberty is large to command the attention of everyone who views the harbour.

To be the biggest is an aspiration of landmark developers. Yet it can get confused by the definition of what is big, giving it an advantage over others. To be huge for a reason, gets the landmark higher on the list. If it can add the other factors mentioned, the landmark can win. (See Figure 41: Big is better.)

The Great Landmark Race

The great landmark race is a human-centric race to be legendary in the world, to show, 'we and our creations matter'. The need to visit these landmarks and tick them off our bucket list comes from a desire to experience the best of humanity's endeavours. A landmark is a window into the ambitions and values of the civilisation we are visiting. If it is a temple, cathedral or mosque, built in honour of gods, it tells a story of the importance a particular civilisation places on worship. If it is a tomb, in admiration of a person, it tells us the value this individual has to that civilisation. The tall metal tower in Paris tells a story of ingenuity and technology that the 19th-century French civilisation had to offer the world. It can also represent a moment in time when the United States stood as a beacon for humanity, as expressed in the poem by Emma Lazarus at the base of the Statue of Liberty,

> "Keep, ancient lands, your storied pomp!" cries she
> With silent lips. "Give me your tired, your poor,
> Your huddled masses yearning to breathe free,
> The wretched refuse of your teeming shore.
> Send these, the homeless, tempest-tost to me,
> I lift my lamp beside the golden door!"[98]

In the year 2020, landmarks seem less important than a COVID19 outbreak, than the fight for racial equality rights, or the freedom of a city under a repressive regime. They seem less important, and to many, a waste of money to build. This is factually true. Lives and safety are more important. But they do stand as a reminder of a time. They may be constructed to honour evil leaders and be torn down a few years later, or they can stand for eternity in a desert, like the Pyramid of Giza, challenging the world to be greater than it. When times were bad, it is essential for those days to be remembered, as we do with the gates of Auschwitz, so we do not repeat the horrors. When times are good, a landmark like the Eiffel Tower, built during the roaring industrial revolution, gives humanity a goal to outcompete. We should take the Tower on as a challenge. We should overtake it in the race and be better than it. Humans working together for the common good, to achieve greatness, is a goal all our cities should be competing for. Cities should challenge each other in friendly competition rather than political fighting that pits neighbours, races and nations against each other. Then we should all visit each other, learn about each other's civilisations through our landmarks.

It takes tremendous effort for humanity to come together, financially, as labourers and designers, to create a genuinely spectacular landmark. Many people will fight against its construction. Yet if we only focus on the now, how will future generations remember us?

There will always be counter opinions that will try to stop the creating of world icons. For those trying to get a project to happen against a barrier of pessimists, I offer a lesson from the world's greatest landmark, the Eiffel Tower. Tell them it is temporary. If it is loved, it will stay, and if it is hated, it will go away. Build it... and let time sort it out.

Figure 42: The Eiffel Tower, Paris.

The Ranking

Rank	Landmark	Location	Country	Category	Rating
1	Eiffel Tower	Paris	France	Tower	26.69
2	Sagrada Familia	Barcelona	Spain	Church/Mosque	24.47
3	Colosseum	Rome	Italy	Arena	24.28
4	Taj Mahal	Agra	India	Memorial/Monument	23.30
5	Acropolis	Athens	Greece	Mountain Complex	22.73
6	Hagia Sophia	Istanbul	Turkey	Church/Mosque	22.39
7	Cathedral Santa Maria di Fiore	Florence	Italy	Church/Mosque	21.61
8	Machu Picchu	Cusco	Peru	Mountain Complex	21.56
9	Pyramids of Giza	El Gizeh	Egypt	Tomb	21.48
10	St Basil's Cathedral	Moscow	Russia	Church/Mosque	21.46
11	Golden Gate Bridge	San Francisco	United States of America	Bridge	21.26
12	Statue of Liberty	New York City	United States of America	Statue/Sculpture	21.04
13	Mont Saint Michel	Saint Michel	France	Mountain Complex	20.82
14	Christ the Redeemer	Rio de Janeiro	Brazil	Statue/Sculpture	20.52
15	Neuschwanstein Castle	Hohenschwangau	Germany	Castle/Palace	20.48
16	Shwedagon Pagoda	Yangon	Myanmar	Temple/Shrine	20.27
17	Great Wall of China	Badaling Area	China	Wall/Gate	20.16
18	Notre Dame de Paris	Paris	France	Church/Mosque	20.14
19	Bayon Temple at Angkor	Angkor Wat	Cambodia	Temple/Shrine	19.94

Rank	Landmark	Location	Country	Category	Rating
20	Big Ben	London	United Kingdom	Other	19.77
21	Sydney Opera House	Sydney	Australia	Cultural/ Arts Museum	19.61
22	Louvre	Paris	France	Cultural/ Arts Museum	19.48
23	Rialto Bridge	Venice	Italy	Bridge	19.29
24	Blue Mosque	Istanbul	Turkey	Church/ Mosque	19.01
25	Cradle Mountain	Tasmania, Central Highlands	Australia	Mountain	19.00
26	Uluru	Northern Territory	Australia	Natural Feature	18.99
27	St Peters Basilica	Vatican City	Italy	Church/ Mosque	18.96
28	Brooklyn Bridge	New York City	United States of America	Bridge	18.94
29	Our Saviour on Spilled Blood	Saint Petersburg	Russia	Church/ Mosque	18.94
30	Meteora	Thessaly	Greece	Mountain Complex	18.87
31	Kremlin	Moscow	Russia	Political	18.85
32	Potala Palace	Lhasa, Tibet	China	Castle/ Palace	18.67
33	Leaning Tower of Pisa	Pisa	Italy	Tall Building	18.62
34	Itsukushima-Jinja gate	Itsukushima	Japan	Statue/ Sculpture	18.48
35	St Mark's Campanile and Piazza San Marco	Venice	Italy	Park/Plaza	18.48
36	Empire State Building	New York City	United States of America	Tall Building	18.47
37	Chartres Cathedral	Chartres	France	Church/ Mosque	18.31

Rank	Landmark	Location	Country	Category	Rating
38	Burj Al Arab	Dubai	United Arab Republic	Tall Building	18.25
39	Charles Bridge	Prague	Czech Republic	Bridge	18.16
40	Château Frontenac	Québec	Canada	Other	18.05
41	Prague Castle	Prague	Czech Republic	Castle/Palace	17.97
42	Forbidden City Meridian Gate	Beijing	China	Wall/Gate	17.95
43	Boudhanath Stupa	Kathmandu	Nepal	Temple/Shrine	17.90
44	Cologne Cathedral	Cologne	Germany	Church/Mosque	17.87
45	Dome of the Rock	Jerusalem	Israel	Church/Mosque	17.86
46	Sydney Harbour Bridge	Sydney	Australia	Bridge	17.80
47	Shwezigon Pagoda	Bagan	Myanmar	Temple/Shrine	17.72
48	Tower Bridge	London	United Kingdom	Bridge	17.55
49	Trevi Fountain	Rome	Italy	Waterbody	17.47
50	London Eye	London	United Kingdom	Other	17.46
51	Pantheon	Rome	Italy	Church/Mosque	17.41
52	Great Buddha	Kamakura	Japan	Statue/Sculpture	17.25
53	Ponte Vecchio	Florence	Italy	Bridge	17.20
54	Saints Peter and Paul Cathedral	Peterhof	Russia	Church/Mosque	17.17
55	Grand Buddha	Leshan	China	Memorial/Monument	17.03
56	Minaret of Jam	Shahrak District	Afghanistan	Tower	17.00
57	Kiev Pechersk Lavra	Kiev	Ukraine	Monastery	17.00
58	Angel Falls	Canaima National Park	Venezuela	Natural Feature	16.97

© Christopher J. Elliott

Rank	Landmark	Location	Country	Category	Rating
59	Taipei 101	Taipei	Taiwan	Tall Building	16.95
60	Matterhorn	Zermatt	Switzerland	Mountain	16.93
61	Pyramids of Teotihuacan	Teotihuacan	Mexico	Tomb	16.93
62	Burj Khalifa	Dubai	United Arab Republic	Tall Building	16.91
63	Capitol Hill	Washington DC	United States of America	Political	16.90
64	Ishak Pasha Palace	Doğubeyazıt	Turkey	Castle/Palace	16.81
65	Jaisalmer	Rajasthan	India	Castle/Palace	16.80
66	Pont Du Gard	Vers-Pont-du-Gard	France	Bridge	16.78
67	Ananda Temple	Bagan	Myanmar	Temple/Shrine	16.75
68	Segovia's Acueducto	Segovia	Spain	Other	16.73
69	Sugarloaf Mountain	Rio de Janeiro	Brazil	Mountain	16.73
70	Virupaksha Temple	Hampi	India	Temple/Shrine	16.67
71	CN Tower	Toronto	Canada	Tower	16.63
72	Pyramid of Chichen Itza	Yucatan State	Mexico	Temple/Shrine	16.51
73	Edinburgh Castle	Edinburgh	United Kingdom	Castle /Palace	16.50
74	Arc de Triomphe	Paris	France	Memorial/Monument	16.49
75	Mount Fuji	Yamanashi and Shizuoka	Japan	Mountain	16.48
76	Dhammayangyi Temple	Bagan	Myanmar	Temple/Shrine	16.47
77	Borobudur Temple Compounds	Magelang	Indonesia	Temple/Shrine	16.47
78	Tokyo Tower	Tokyo	Japan	Tower	16.47
79	Temple IV Calakmul Ruins	Campeche	Mexico	Memorial/Monument	16.45

Rank	Landmark	Location	Country	Category	Rating
80	Palace of Versailles	Versailles	France	Castle/Palace	16.43
81	Karlstejn Castle	Karlstejn	Czech Republic	Castle/Palace	16.43
82	Zocalo	Mexico City	Mexico	Park/Plaza	16.37
83	Tower of Buddhist Incense Summer Palace	Beijing	China	Temple/Shrine	16.36
84	Millau Viaduct	Creissels	France	Bridge	16.31
85	Tian Tan Buddha	Lantau Island	Hong Kong	Statue/Sculpture	16.29
86	Sphinx of Giza	Giza	Egypt	Statue/Sculpture	16.24
87	Tikal Temple	Flores, Petén	Guatemala	Memorial/Monument	16.24
88	Kalon Minaret	Bukhara	Uzbekistan	Church/Mosque	16.21
89	Siena Cathedral (Piazza Del Campo)	Siena	Italy	Church/Mosque	16.17
90	Uffizi	Florence	Italy	Cultural/Arts Museum	16.12
91	Hermitage (Winter Palace)	Saint Petersburg	Russia	Castle/Palace	16.07
92	Sigiriya	Dambulla	Sri Lanka	Mountain Complex	15.97
93	Forbidden City	Beijing	China	Castle/Palace	15.96
94	Newgrange	Boyne	Ireland	Memorial/Monument	15.92
95	Alhambra	Granada	Spain	Castle/Palace	15.91
96	Skellig Michael	County Kerry	Ireland	Natural Feature	15.85
97	Sheikh Zayed Grand Mosque	Abu Dhabi	United Arab Republic	Church/Mosque	15.79
98	Alcatraz	San Francisco	United States of America	Other	15.75

Rank	Landmark	Location	Country	Category	Rating
99	Paro Taktsang	Paro District	Bhutan	Mountain Complex	15.74
100	Willis Tower	Chicago	United States of America	Tall Building	15.73
101	Mosque-Cathedral of Cordoba	Mezquita	Spain	Church/Mosque	15.71
102	Guggenheim Museum	Bilbao	Spain	Cultural/Arts Museum	15.70
103	Hollywood Sign	Hollywood	United States of America	Big Attraction	15.67
104	Westminster Abbey	London	United Kingdom	Church/Mosque	15.65
105	Basilique du Sacre-Coeur de Montmartre	Paris	France	Church/Mosque	15.63
106	Bourges Cathedral	Bourges	France	Church/Mosque	15.59
107	Alexander Nevsky Cathedral	Tallinn	Estonia	Church/Mosque	15.57
108	Pena Palace	Sintra	Portugal	Castle/Palace	15.54
109	Petronas Towers	Kuala Lumpur	Malaysia	Tall Building	15.54
110	Himeji Castle	Himeji	Japan	Castle/Palace	15.53
111	Caernarfon Castle	Wales	United Kingdom	Castle/Palace	15.51
112	Canterbury Cathedral	Canterbury	United Kingdom	Church/Mosque	15.47
113	Stonehenge	Wiltshire	United Kingdom	Memorial/Monument	15.45
114	Oceanographic Museum	Monaco	Monaco	Cultural/Arts Museum	15.44
115	Fortress Hohensalzburg	Salzburg	Austria	Castle/Palace	15.43

Rank	Landmark	Location	Country	Category	Rating
116	Titanic Belfast	Northern Ireland	United Kingdom	Cultural/Arts Museum	15.42
117	Punakha Dzong	Punakha	Bhutan	Temple/Shrine	15.42
118	Washington Monument	Washington	United States of America	Memorial/Monument	15.39
119	Brussels' Grand Place	Brussels	Belgium	Castle/Palace	15.37
120	Mogao Caves	Dunhuang	China	Temple/Shrine	15.36
121	One World Trade Center (Freedom tower)	New York City	United States of America	Tall Building	15.34
122	Atomium	Brussels	Belgium	Statue/Sculpture	15.31
123	Shanghai World Financial Center	Shanghai	China	Tall Building	15.31
124	Hungarian Parliament Building	Budapest	Hungary	Political	15.30
125	Naqsh-e Jahan	Isfahan	Iran	Park/Plaza	15.22
126	St Olaf's church	Tallinn	Estonia	Church/Mosque	15.22
127	Palace of Westminster	London	United Kingdom	Political	15.20
128	Kilimanjaro	Kilimanjaro	Tanzania	Mountain	15.16
129	Tower of London	London	United Kingdom	Tall Building	15.09
130	Dubrovnik Old City Walls	Dubrovnik	Croatia	Wall/Gate	15.06
131	Aiguille du Midi	French Alps	France	Mountain	15.05
132	Lotus Temple	New Delhi	India	Temple/Shrine	15.02
133	Capital Gate	Abu Dhabi	United Arab Emirates	Tall Building	14.98
134	Kronborg Castle	Helsingør	Denmark	Castle/Palace	14.94
135	Reichstag	Berlin	Germany	Political	14.93

Rank	Landmark	Location	Country	Category	Rating
136	Mosque–Cathedral of Córdoba	Córdoba	Spain	Church/Mosque	14.88
137	Vatican	Vatican City	Vatican City	Tall Building	14.86
138	Victoria Falls	Zambia	Zimbabwe	Waterbody	14.86
139	Konark Sun Temple	Konark	India	Temple/Shrine	14.81
140	Tate Modern	London	United Kingdom	Cultural/Arts Museum	14.80
141	Metropolitan Cathedral of Brasília	Brasília	Brazil	Church/Mosque	14.76
142	Duomo di Milano	Milan	Italy	Tall Building	14.74
143	Oslo Opera House	Oslo	Norway	Cultural/Arts Museum	14.73
144	Château de Chambord	Chambord	France	Castle/Palace	14.71
145	Faisal Mosque	Islamabad	Pakistan	Church/Mosque	14.70
146	Shard (The)	London	United Kingdom	Tall Building	14.70
147	Lincoln Memorial	Washington	United States of America	Memorial/Monument	14.63
148	Chrysler Building	New York City	United States of America	Tall Building	14.62
149	Swiss Re Building (Gherkin)	London	United Kingdom	Tall Building	14.55
150	Palenque	Chiapas	Mexico	Memorial/Monument	14.49
151	Brandenburg Gate	Berlin	Germany	Wall/Gate	14.48
152	La Citadelle la Ferriere	Nord	Haiti	Fort	14.47
153	Berlin Cathedral	Berlin	Germany	Church/Mosque	14.44
154	Amphitheatre of El Jem	El Djem	Tunisia	Arena	14.41

Rank	Landmark	Location	Country	Category	Rating
155	Pentagon	Arlington	United States of America	Political	14.41
156	Space Needle	Seattle	United States of America	Tower	14.40
157	Shwesandaw Pagoda	Bagan	Myanmar	Temple/Shrine	14.37
158	Table Mountain	Cape Town	South Africa	Mountain	14.36
159	Great Theatre	Ephesus	Turkey	Arena	14.36
160	Sleeping Beauty's Castle	Disney Worlds Magic Kingdom	United States of America	Other	14.35
161	Château de Chenonceau	Loire Valley	France	Castle/Palace	14.33
162	Bra na Boinne	County Meath	Ireland	Tomb	14.30
163	Rock of Cashel	County Tipperary	Ireland	Castle/Palace	14.27
164	Santiago de Compostela Cathedral	Galicia	Spain	Church/Mosque	14.26
165	St Pauls Cathedral	London	United Kingdom	Church/Mosque	14.25
166	Ahu Ature Huki	Easter Island	Chile	Statue/Sculpture	14.21
167	Bran Castle	Brașov	Romania	Castle/Palace	14.20
168	Town Hall Tower	Krakow	Poland	Tower	14.17
169	Registan Square	Samarkand city	Uzbekistan	Park/Plaza	14.16
170	Mount Etna	Catania	Italy	Mountain	14.14
171	Gros Piton	Southwest	Saint Lucia	Mountain	14.07
172	Griffith Observatory	Los Angeles	United States of America	Other	14.07
173	Heydar Aliyev Cultural Centre	Baku	Azerbaijan	Cultural/Arts Museum	14.07

Rank	Landmark	Location	Country	Category	Rating
174	Kizhi Pogost	Lake Onega	Russia	Church/Mosque	14.06
175	Melk Abbey	Melk	Austria	Church/Mosque	13.95
176	Schwerin Castle	Schwerin	Germany	Castle/Palace	13.92
177	Lahore Fort	Lahore	Pakistan	Fort	13.88
178	White House	Washington D.C.	United States of America	Political	13.87
179	Stari Most	Mostar	Bosnia and Herzegovina	Bridge	13.86
180	Musée d'Orsay	Paris	France	Cultural/Arts Museum	13.85
181	Gateway Arch	Saint Louis	USA	Memorial/Monument	13.85
182	Niterói Contemporary Art Museum	Niterói	Brazil	Cultural/Arts Museum	13.84
183	The Guggenheim	New York City	USA	Cultural/Arts Museum	13.82
184	Gardens by the Bay	Marina	Singapore	Other	13.80
185	Trakai Castle	Trakai	Lithuania	Castle/Palace	13.78
186	Papal Palace	Avignon	France	Castle/Palace	13.77
187	Moulin Rouge	Paris	France	Other	13.77
188	Great Mosque of Mecca	Mecca	Saudi Arabia	Church/Mosque	13.76
189	Eiger	Bernese	Switzerland	Mountain	13.76
190	Lion on the Mound	Waterloo	Belgium	Statue/Sculpture	13.72
191	Dormition of the Mother of God Church	Mănăstirea Humorului	Romania	Church/Mosque	13.72
192	Chapel Bridge (Kapellbrücke)	Lucerne	Switzerland	Bridge	13.70

Rank	Landmark	Location	Country	Category	Rating
193	Spis Castle	spišská nová ves	Slovakia	Castle/Palace	13.69
194	Mount Rushmore	Black Hills	United States of America	Statue/Sculpture	13.68
195	Three Towers Torres del Paine	Magallanes	Chile	Mountain	13.67
196	Mosteiro Dos Jeronimos	Lisbon	Portugal	Cultural/Arts Museum	13.65
197	Galle Fort Lighthouse		Sri Lanka	Tower	13.62
198	St Nicholas Church	Probota	Romania	Church/Mosque	13.62
199	Vienna Opera House	Vienna	Austria	Cultural/Arts Museum	13.61
200	Victoria Peak	Hong Kong Island	Hong Kong	Mountain	13.55
201	Cloud Gate	Chicago	United States of America	Statue/Sculpture	13.53
202	Petra	Ma'an	Jordan	Statue/Sculpture	13.52
203	Grand Palace	Bangkok	Thailand	Castle/Palace	13.45
204	Windsor Castle	Windsor	United Kingdom	Castle/Palace	13.44
205	Stupa Swayambhunath	Kathmandu	Nepal	Temple/Shrine	13.44
206	York Minster	York	United Kingdom	Church/Mosque	13.42
207	Ellis Island Museum of Immigration	New York	United States of America	Cultural/Arts Museum	13.40
208	Carcassonne Walled City	Carcassonne	France	Castle/Palace	13.39
209	National Museum of Anthropology	Manila	Philippines	Cultural/Arts Museum	13.36
210	Mount Vesuvius	Campania	Italy	Mountain	13.32

Rank	Landmark	Location	Country	Category	Rating
211	Mount Kenya	Central Kenya	Kenya	Mountain	13.32
212	Amber Fort	Amer	India	Fort	13.29
213	Japanese Covered Bridge in Hoi An	Hoi An	Vietnam	Bridge	13.29
214	St George Church	Voroneț	Romania	Church/Mosque	13.29
215	Amalienborg Palace	Copenhagen	Denmark	Castle/Palace	13.27
216	Meenakshi Amman Temple	Tamil Nadu	India	Temple/Shrine	13.27
217	Wailing Wall	Jerusalem	Israel	Wall/Gate	13.26
218	National Palace Museum	Taipei	Taiwan	Castle/Palace	13.24
219	Djenne Mosque	Mopti	Mali	Church/Mosque	13.23
220	Fatehpur Sikri	Agra	India	Temple/Shrine	13.21
221	Middle of the World (Ciudad Mitad del Mundo)	Quito	Ecuador	Memorial/Monument	13.20
222	Rock of Gibraltar		Gibraltar	Mountain	13.20
223	Kinkaku-ji	Kyoto	Japan	Temple/Shrine	13.16
224	Three Sisters	Blue Mountains National Park	Australia	Natural Feature	13.12
225	Arena Di Verona	Verona	Italy	Arena	13.11
226	Thiksey Monastery	Lhasa	Tibet	Monastery	13.10
227	Dalí Theatre and Museum	Catalonia	Spain	Cultural/Arts Museum	13.09
228	Karnak	Luxor	Egypt	Temple/Shrine	13.09
229	Golden Temple	Amritsar	India	Temple/Shrine	13.07
230	Volcan Arenal	Alajuela Province	Costa Rica	Mountain	13.04

Rank	Landmark	Location	Country	Category	Rating
231	Eden Project	Cornwall	United Kingdom	Other	13.04
232	Bamburgh Castle	Bamburge	United Kingdom	Castle/ Palace	13.04
233	Széchenyi Thermal Baths	Budapest	Hungary	Waterbody	13.00
234	Mount Kailash	Tibet	China	Mountain	13.00
235	Geysir	Haukadalsvegur	Iceland	Other	12.99
236	Pompidou Centre	Paris	France	Cultural/ Arts Museum	12.97
237	Royal Palace of Madrid	Madrid	Spain	Castle/ Palace	12.96
238	Mill Network	Alblasserwaard polder	Netherlands	Industrial	12.94
239	Helsinki Cathedral	Helsinki	Finland	Church/ Mosque	12.91
240	Rila Monastery	Rila Mountains	Bulgaria	Monastery	12.91
241	Dresden Frauenkirche	Dresden	Germany	Church/ Mosque	12.90
242	Concepcion (Volcano)	Isla de Ometepe	Nicaragua	Mountain	12.89
243	Hiroshima Peace Memorial	Hiroshima	Japan	Memorial/ Monument	12.87
244	Wat Phou	Champasak	Laos	Temple/ Shrine	12.85
245	Sphinx in Bucegi	Bucegi	Romania	Natural Feature	12.83
246	Mansudae Grand Monument	Pyongyang	North Korea	Statue/ Sculpture	12.77
247	Catherine Palace	St Petersburg	Russia	Castle/ Palace	12.77
248	Rijksmuseum	Amsterdam	Netherlands	Cultural/ Arts Museum	12.76
249	Exaltation of the Holy Cross Church	Pătrăuți	Romania	Church/ Mosque	12.76
250	Avebury Stone Circle	Wiltshire	United Kingdom	Memorial/ Monument	12.72

Rank	Landmark	Location	Country	Category	Rating
251	White Cliffs of Dover	Dover	United Kingdom	Natural Feature	12.71
252	Confucius Temple	Qufu	China	Temple/Shrine	12.68
253	Temple of Bacchus	Baalbek	Lebanon	Temple/Shrine	12.68
254	The Flatiron Building	New York City	United States of America	Tall Building	12.63
255	Natural History Museum	London	United Kingdom	Cultural/Arts Museum	12.63
256	Metropolitan Museum of Art	New York City	United States of America	Cultural/Arts Museum	12.62
257	Bled Island	Julian Alps	Slovenia	Other	12.62
258	São Paulo Museum of Art	São Paulo	Brazil	Cultural/Arts Museum	12.58
259	N Seoul Tower	Seoul	South Korea	Tower	12.57
260	Malbork Castle	Malbork	Poland	Castle/Palace	12.57
261	Nizwa Fort	Nizwa	Oman	Fort	12.55
262	Iguazu Falls	Misiones	Brazil	Natural Feature	12.54
263	Temple of the God of Wind	Tulum	Mexico	Temple/Shrine	12.54
264	Mount Everest	Sagarmatha National Park	Nepal	Mountain	12.52
265	Mount Eden Crater	Auckland	New Zealand	Mountain	12.52
266	Casa Mila	Barcelona	Spain	Residential	12.48
267	Plaza De Espana	Seville	Spain	Park/Plaza	12.47
268	Schilthorn	Bernese Alps	Switzerland	Mountain Complex	12.43
269	Abu Simbel	Upper Egypt	Egypt	Temple/Shrine	12.42
270	Museo del Prado	Madrid	Spain	Cultural/Arts Museum	12.42

Rank	Landmark	Location	Country	Category	Rating
271	Veliki slap	Plitvice Lakes National Park	Croatia	Waterbody	12.41
272	Ostrog Monastery	Bjelopavlići	Montenegro	Mountain Complex	12.39
273	British Museum	London	United Kingdom	Cultural/ Arts Museum	12.38
274	The Penitentiary	Port Arthur	Australia	Other	12.33
275	Beit She'an	Northern District	Israel	Arena	12.29
276	Tsarskoe Selo	St Petersburg	Russia	Castle/ Palace	12.28
277	Wat Phra Si Sanphet	Ayutthaya	Thailand	Temple/ Shrine	12.25
278	Niagara Falls	Ontario, New York State	Canada, United States of America	Natural Feature	12.19
279	Mount Roraima		Venezuela	Mountain	12.18
280	Kirkjufell	Snaefellsnes	Iceland	Mountain	12.17
281	Changdeokgung Palace	Changdeokgung	South Korea	Castle/ Palace	12.15
282	Topkapi Palace	Instanbul	Turkey	Castle/ Palace	12.14
283	Mount Ararat	Ağrı provinces	Turkey	Mountain	12.13
284	St David's Cathedral	Wales	United Kingdom	Church/ Mosque	12.12
285	Ko Tapu	Phang Nga Bay	Thailand	Natural Feature	12.12
286	Fort d'Estrées	Gorée Island	Senegal	Fort	12.11
287	Giant's Causeway	County Antrim	United Kingdom	Natural Feature	12.08
288	Trinity College	Cambridge	United Kingdom	Education	12.08

Rank	Landmark	Location	Country	Category	Rating
289	Columbia Icefield Skywalk	Jasper National Park	Canada	Other	12.05
290	Casino de Monte Carlo	Monte Carlo	Monaco	Other	12.02
291	Semperoper	Dresden	Germany	Cultural/ Arts Museum	12.01
292	Museum of Old and New Art	Hobart	Australia	Tall Building	11.98
293	Te Papa Tongarewa	Wellington	New Zealand	Cultural/ Arts Museum	11.98
294	Cerro Fitz Roy	Southern Patagonia	Chile	Mountain	11.89
295	Temple of Besakih	Bali	Indonesia	Temple/ Shrine	11.88
296	Temppeliaukio Kirkko	Helsinki	Finland	Church/ Mosque	11.85
297	Mount Kinabalu	Sabah	Malaysia	Mountain	11.83
298	Egyptian Museum	Cairo	Egypt	Cultural/ Arts Museum	11.80
299	Villa Savoye	Poissy	France	Residential	11.79
300	Mount McKinley	Alaska	United States of America	Mountain	11.78
301	Ben Nevis	Lochaber	United Kingdom	Mountain	11.74
302	Oxford University	Oxford	United Kingdom	Education	11.73
303	Stirling Castle	Scotland	United Kingdom	Church/ Mosque	11.72
304	Luxor Temple	Luxor	Egypt	Temple/ Shrine	11.67
305	Jokhang Temple	Tibet	China	Temple/ Shrine	11.66
306	Piton de la Fournaise	East Reunion Ilsand	Reunion	Mountain	11.64

Rank	Landmark	Location	Country	Category	Rating
307	Lincoln Center	New York City	United States of America	Cultural/ Arts Museum	11.60
308	Camp Nou	Barcelona	Spain	Arena	11.60
309	Buckingham Palace	London	United Kingdom	Castle/ Palace	11.57
310	Mont Blanc	Alps	France	Mountain	11.54
311	Van Gogh Museum	Amsterdam	Netherlands	Cultural/ Arts Museum	11.52
312	Colossi of Memnon	Valley of the Kings	Egypt	Memorial/ Monument	11.50
313	Kelvingrove Art Gallery and Museum	Glasgow	United Kingdom	Cultural/ Arts Museum	11.50
314	Temple of the Tooth	Kandy	Sri Lanka	Temple/ Shrine	11.45
315	Erdene Zuu Khiid	Kharkhorin	Mongolia	Temple/ Shrine	11.37
316	Al Aqsa Mosque	Jerusalem	Israel & Palestine	Church/ Mosque	11.35
317	Mount Sinai	Sinai Peninsula	Egypt	Mountain	11.31
318	Anne Frank House	Amsterdam	Netherlands	Tall Building	11.21
319	Trajan's Arch	Batna Province	Algeria	Wall/Gate	11.19
320	Khaju Bridge	Isfahan	Iran	Bridge	11.16
321	Iona Abbey	Isle of Iona	United Kingdom	Church/ Mosque	11.15
322	Jungfraujoch	Bernese Alps	Switzerland	Mountain	11.12
323	Choquequirao	Santa Teresa	Peru	Mountain Complex	11.09
324	Caracol	Cayo District	Belize	Temple/ Shrine	11.07
325	Wat Rong Khun	Chiang Rai	Thailand	Temple/ Shrine	11.06
326	Blue domed Church	Santorini	Greece	Church/ Mosque	11.06
327	Temple of the Masonry Altars	Altun Ha	Belize	Temple/ Shrine	11.06

Rank	Landmark	Location	Country	Category	Rating
328	Tintern Abbey	Tintern	United Kingdom	Church/Mosque	11.02
329	Gate of All Nations	Persepolis	Iran	Wall/Gate	10.91
330	Twelve Apostles	Victoria	Australia	Natural Feature	10.89
331	Great Zimbabwe National Monument	Masvingo Province	Zimbabwe	Memorial/Monument	10.87
332	Kalemegdan	Belgrade	Serbia	Castle/Palace	10.84
333	Bryggen	Bergen	Norway	Other	10.79
334	Times Square	New York City	United States of America	Park/Plaza	10.73
335	Blue Lagoon (geothermal spa)	Grindavík	Iceland	Waterbody	10.64
336	Piccadilly Circus	London	United Kingdom	Park/Plaza	10.63
337	Cape Coast Castle	McCarthy Hill	Ghana	Fort	10.55
338	Gold Museum	Bogotá	Colombia	Cultural/Arts Museum	10.52
339	Dancing House	Prague	Czech Republic	Residential	10.51
340	Auschwitz Entrance Gate	Auschwitz	Poland	Other	10.48
341	Dashashwamedh Ghat	Varanasi	India	Other	10.40
342	David Gareja monastery complex	Kakheti Region	Georgia	Mountain Complex	10.34
343	MuseumsQuartier	Vienna	Austria	Park/Plaza	10.31
344	Grouse Mountain	Vancouver	Canada	Mountain	10.26
345	Spanish Steps	Rome	Italy	Park/Plaza	10.21
346	Art Institute of Chicago	Chicago	United States of America	Cultural/Arts Museum	10.21
347	Berlin Wall	Berlin	Germany	Wall/Gate	10.14

Rank	Landmark	Location	Country	Category	Rating
348	Little Mermaid	Copenhagen	Denmark	Statue/Sculpture	10.05
349	Gullfoss	South West Iceland	Iceland	Waterbody	9.95
350	Vinson Massif	Sentinel Range	Antarctica	Mountain	9.95
351	Plaza Mayor	Madrid	Spain	Park/Plaza	9.92
352	Durbar Square	Kathmandu Valley	Nepal	Park/Plaza	9.87
353	Pulpit Rock	Rogaland	Norway	Natural Feature	9.81
354	Fallingwater	Mill Run	United States of America	Residential	9.69
355	Graceland	Memphis	United States of America	Residential	9.35
356	Standing Stones of Callanish	Lewis	Scotland	Memorial/Monument	9.33
357	Shibuya Crossing	Tokyo	Japan	Other	9.27
358	Bardo National Museum	Tunis	Tunisia	Cultural/Arts Museum	9.25
359	Zwinger	Dresden	Germany	Castle/Palace	9.13
360	Moraine Lake	Banff National Park	Canada	Waterbody	9.06
361	Murchison Falls	Victoria Nile	Uganda	Waterbody	8.90
362	St Fagans National History Museum	Cardiff	United Kingdom	Cultural/Arts Museum	8.89
363	Museu Picasso	Barcelona	Spain	Cultural/Arts Museum	8.82
364	Kigali Memorial Centre	Kigali	Rwanda	Memorial/Monument	8.78
365	Shackleton's Hut	Cape Royds	Antarctica	Residential	8.62
366	Church of Sveti Jovan Bigorski	Mavrovo	Macedonian	Church/Mosque	8.32

Rank	Landmark	Location	Country	Category	Rating
367	L'Anse aux Meadows	Newfoundland	Canada	Memorial/Monument	8.09
368	Normandy American Cemetery and Memorial	Colleville-sur-Mer	France	Memorial/Monument	7.53

Bibliography

1. Lock, S. *Tourism worldwide - Statistics & Facts*. 2020 [cited 2020 20/04]; Available from: https://www.statista.com/topics/962/global-tourism/.
2. Smith, K. *Everything We Know About The Isolated Sentinelese People Of North Sentinel Island*. 2018 [cited 2020 19/05]; Available from: https://www.forbes.com/sites/kionasmith/2018/11/30/everything-we-know-about-the-isolated-sentinelese-people-of-north-sentinel-island/#3b2467c935a0.
3. Weber, G., *Lonely islands : the Andamanese : bibliography / by George Weber*. 1998, Liestal, Switzerland: The Andaman Association.
4. Deloitte, *How do you value an icon? The Sydney Opera House: economic, cultural and digital value*. 2013.
5. Kanopy, *Iguazu Falls-Thundering Waterfalls*. 2015, San Francisco, California, USA : Kanopy Streaming.
6. Lonely Planet, *Ultimate Travel List*. 2015: Lonely Planet Publications Pty Ltd.
7. Graff, R. *Top 10 Famous Landmarks In The World*. 2019 [cited 2019 13/04]; Available from: https://www.kids-world-travel-guide.com/top-10-famous-landmarks.html.
8. Oxford. *The English Oxford Dictionary*. 2018 [cited 2019 9/12]; Available from: https://en.oxforddictionaries.com/definition/landmark.

9. McLean, R., *The Geomorphology of the Great Barrier Reef: Development, Diversity and Change - by David Hopley, Scott G. Smithers and Kevin E. Parnell*. 2009: Melbourne, Australia. p. 87-89.
10. Google Inc. *Google Trends*. 2020 [cited 2020 3/05]; Available from: https://trends.google.com/trends.
11. Florida, R. *Sorry, London: New York Is the World's Most Economically Powerful City*. 2015 [cited 2020 3/05]; Available from: https://www.citylab.com/life/2015/03/sorry-london-new-york-is-the-worlds-most-economically-powerful-city/386315/.
12. Wedesweiler, M. *Take a look at seven of the smallest towns in the world*. 2016 [cited 2020 3/05]; Available from: https://www.domain.com.au/news/take-a-look-at-seven-of-the-smallest-towns-in-the-world-20161021-gs5yzf/.
13. ABC News. *A Danish architect, an Australian icon: the history of the Sydney Opera House*. 2013 [cited 2020 03/05]; Available from: https://www.abc.net.au/news/2013-10-21/anthony-burke-on-sydney-opera-house-history/5034028.
14. The Arts Centre Melbourne. *Our History*. 2019 [cited 2020 3/05]; Available from: https://www.artscentremelbourne.com.au/about-us/our-history.
15. Victoria, P.R.O. *Missing the Mark- What Federation Square could have been*. 2011 [cited 2020 26/04]; Available from: https://prov.vic.gov.au/about-us/our-blog/missing-mark.

16. City of Yarra, *22.03 Landmarks and tall structures*. 2019.
17. Coward, N., *Collected sketches and lyrics*. 1931, London: London : Hutchinson.
18. Abadi, M. *Trump had an unusual reaction to 9/11 just hours after the attacks*. 2017 [cited 2020 26/06]; Available from: https://www.businessinsider.com.au/trump-september-11-interview-tallest-building-manhattan-2017-9.
19. Council of Tall Buildings and Urban Habitat (CTBUH). *CTBUH Height Criteria*. 2020 [cited 2020 1/05]; Available from: https://www.ctbuh.org/resource/height.
20. Diamond, J.M., *Guns, germs and steel : the fates of human societies / Jared Diamond*. 1997, London: Jonathan Cape.
21. German, D.S. *White Temple and ziggurat, Uruk*. 2020 [cited 2020 27/04]; Available from: https://www.khanacademy.org/humanities/ap-art-history/ancient-mediterranean-ap/ancient-near-east-a/a/white-temple-and-ziggurat-uruk.
22. Jarus, O. *Step Pyramid of Djoser: Egypt's First Pyramid*. 2012 [cited 2020 28/04]; Available from: https://www.livescience.com/23050-step-pyramid-djoser.html.
23. Kinnaer, J. *Meidum Pyramid*. The Ancient Egypt Site 2014 [cited 2020 28/04]; Available from: http://www.ancient-egypt.org/history/old-kingdom/4th-dynasty/snofru/pyramids/meidum-pyramid.html.
24. Kinnaer, J. *Bent Pyramid at Dashur*. The Ancient Egypt Site 2014 [cited 2020 28/04];

Available from: http://www.ancient-egypt.org/history/old-kingdom/4th-dynasty/snofru/pyramids/bent-pyramid-at-dashur.html.

25. Hamilton, K., *The Red Pyramid. A layman's guide*. 2017.
26. Kinnaer, J. *Red Pyramid at Dashur*. The Ancient Egypt Site 2014 [cited 2020 28/04]; Available from: http://www.ancient-egypt.org/history/old-kingdom/4th-dynasty/snofru/pyramids/red-pyramid-at-dashur.html.
27. Rawlinson, K. *New discovery throws light on mystery of pyramids' construction*. 2018 [cited 2020 28/04]; Available from: https://www.theguardian.com/world/2018/nov/06/new-discovery-throws-light-on-mystery-of-pyramids-construction.
28. NOVA. *Who Built the Pyramids?* 1997 [cited 2020 29/06]; Available from: https://www.pbs.org/wgbh/nova/article/who-built-the-pyramids/.
29. Abernethy, S. *Old St. Paul's Cathedral of London*. 2014 [cited 2020 28/04]; Available from: https://www.medievalists.net/2014/04/old-st-pauls-cathedral-london/.
30. Staff, N.C. *10 fascinating facts about the Washington Monument*. 2019 [cited 2020 29/04]; Available from: https://constitutioncenter.org/blog/10-fascinating-facts-about-the-washington-monument.

31. Heyman, S., *Paris Raises Its Silhouette, but Slowly and Not Easily*, in *The New York Times*. 2015.
32. Young, M. *Top 10 Secrets of the Chrysler Building in NYC*. 2015 [cited 2020 30/04]; Available from: https://untappedcities.com/2015/02/19/top-10-secrets-of-the-chrysler-building-in-nyc/2/.
33. OpieRadio, *Opie walking talking in nyc #11 - Climbing to top of Chrysler Building Spire*. 2013, YouTube.
34. Photos, R.H. *Named by Life magazine as the "The Most Beautiful Suicide" - Evelyn McHale leapt to her death from the Empire State Building, 1947*. 2014 [cited 2020 30/04]; Available from: https://rarehistoricalphotos.com/beautiful-suicide-evelyn-mchale-leapt-death-empire-state-building-1947/.
35. 9 News Oklahoma, *End of An Era: KWTV To Take Down Historic Broadcast Tower*. 2014.
36. Kohlstedt, K. *Unheard Of: The Catastrophic Collapse of the World's Tallest Tower*. 2016 [cited 2020 30/04]; Available from: https://99percentinvisible.org/article/unheard-catastrophic-collapse-worlds-tallest-tower/.
37. Smart, N. *41 Amazing Burj Khalifa Facts*. 2020 [cited 2020 30/04]; Available from: https://hoteljules.com/burj-khalifa-facts/.
38. Properties, E. *The Tower*. 2020 [cited 2020 30/04]; Available from: https://www.burjkhalifa.ae/en/the-tower.
39. Frearson, A. *Foundations for planned "world's tallest building" in China repurposed as fish farm*. 2015 [cited 2020 1/05]; Available from:

https://www.dezeen.com/2015/07/20/foundations-planned-worlds-tallest-building-changsha-china-repurposed-fish-farm-skyscraper-broad-sustainable-building/.

40. McKeown, R. *Jeddah Tower Progress: What Happened to the World's Tallest Tower?* 2020 [cited 2020 1/05]; Available from: https://theurbandeveloper.com/articles/jeddah-tower-progress-update-worlds-tallest-tower.

41. Jacobs, H. *Dubai's glittering, futuristic metropolis came at the cost of hundreds of thousands of workers, and recommending it as a tourist destination feels wrong*. 2018 [cited 2020 01/05]; Available from: https://www.businessinsider.com.au/dubai-development-tourism-workers-problem-2018-12.

42. Yuhas, A., *The Pentagon Released U.F.O. Videos. Don't Hold Your Breath for a Breakthrough.*, in *The New York Times*. 2020.

43. History.com Editors. *Pentagon*. 2009 [cited 2020 10/05]; Available from: https://www.history.com/topics/us-government/pentagon.

44. James, N. *20 Fun Facts About the Hollywood Sign*. 2013 [cited 2020 04/05]; Available from: https://www.signs.com/blog/20-fun-facts-about-the-hollywood-sign/.

45. Munringus. *Lesia. Canora, Saskatchewan*. 2020 [cited 2020 10/05]; Available from: https://www.atlasobscura.com/places/lesia.

46. L, D. *Indian Head Monument*. 2018 [cited 2020 10/05]; Available from: https://www.tripadvisor.com.au/ShowUserReviews-g2242603-d13143659-r558919795-

Indian_Head_Monument-Indian_Head_Saskatchewan.html.
47. Loran, D. *How our Town Got Its Name*. 2020 [cited 2020 10/05]; Available from: https://www.townofindianhead.com/our-history/how-our-town-got-its-name.html.
48. Clarke, A. *Australia's Big Dilemma*. in *SAHANZ 2017 Annual Conference Proceedings*.
49. Dayman, I., *Hopes Big Orange revival could bear fruit for Australia's other 'big things'*, in *ABC News*. 2016.
50. Nikolis, P. *Re-open the Big Orange as a strip club*. 2018 [cited 2020 2/05]; Available from: https://www.change.org/p/berri-barmera-council-re-open-the-big-orange-as-a-strip-club.
51. Le, V., *99 Percent Invisible*, in *Goodness Gracious Great Balls of Twine*. 2019.
52. RoadsideAmerica.com Team. *Long Beach, Washington: World's Largest Spitting Clam*. 2014 [cited 2020 11/05]; Available from: https://www.roadsideamerica.com/tip/1393.
53. Imbler, S. *The Strange Second Life of Ohio's 'Big Basket' Building*. 2019 [cited 2020 4/05]; Available from: https://www.atlasobscura.com/articles/longaberger-basket-building-hotel.
54. History.com Editors. *Statue of Liberty*. 2009 [cited 2020 11/05]; Available from: https://www.history.com/topics/landmarks/statue-of-liberty.
55. UNESCO. *Statue of Liberty*. 1984 [cited 2020 12/05]; Available from: https://whc.unesco.org/en/list/307/.
56. Cascone, S. *Indian Police Have Charged a Cyber-Scammer Who Listed the World's*

Largest Statue for $4 Billion Online as a Bogus Coronavirus Fundraiser. 2020 [cited 2020 12/05]; Available from: https://news.artnet.com/art-world/indian-scammer-worlds-largest-statue-sale-1829910.

57. BusinessToday.In. *Coronavirus fallout: Statue of Unity put up for sale on OLX at Rs 30,000 crore; case filed*. [cited 2020 15/05]; Available from: https://www.businesstoday.in/latest/trends/coronavirus-fallout-statue-of-unity-put-up-for-sale-on-olx-at-rs-30000-crore-case-filed/story/400242.html.

58. UNESCO. *Mount Emei Scenic Area, including Leshan Giant Buddha Scenic Area*. 1996 [cited 2020 12/05]; Available from: https://whc.unesco.org/en/list/779/.

59. Benetton, L. *Today's Art from North Korea*. [cited 2020 11/05]; Available from: https://www.dprk-art.com/.

60. BBC News, *Senegal inaugurates controversial $27m monument*. 2010.

61. Flanagin, J. *These gargantuan North Korean statues can be found all over Africa*. 2015 [cited 2020 11/05]; Available from: https://qz.com/459784/photos-a-brief-tour-of-north-korean-statues-in-africa/.

62. Winter, C., *Mansudae Art Studio, North Korea's Colossal Monument Factory*, in *Bloomberg*. 2013.

63. Slezak, M., *This article is more than 3 years old Australia scrubbed from UN climate change report after government intervention*, in *The Guardian*. 2016.

64. UNESCO. *The Criteria for Selection*. 2019 [cited 2019 19/04]; Available from: https://whc.unesco.org/en/criteria/.
65. UNESCO. *Taj Mahal*. 1983 [cited 2020 13/05]; Available from: https://whc.unesco.org/en/list/252.
66. Kataria, S., *Pollution turns India's white marble Taj Mahal yellow and green*, in *Reuters*. 2018.
67. UNESCO. *San Antonio Missions*. 2015 [cited 2020 13/05]; Available from: https://whc.unesco.org/en/list/1466.
68. UNESCO. *Mogao Caves*. 1987 [cited 2020 13/05]; Available from: https://whc.unesco.org/en/list/440.
69. UNESCO. *Al Qal'a of Beni Hammad*. 1980 [cited 2020 15/05]; Available from: https://whc.unesco.org/en/list/102.
70. Portal to the Heritage of Astronomy. *Category of Astronomical Heritage: tangible immovable Dengfeng observatory, China*. 2020 [cited 2020 13/05]; Available from: https://www3.astronomicalheritage.net/index.php/show-entity?idunescowhc=1305.
71. UNESCO, *Hiroshima Peace Memorial (Genbaku Dome)*. 1996.
72. UNESCO. *Rio de Janeiro: Carioca Landscapes between the Mountain and the Sea*. 2012 [cited 2020 14/05]; Available from: https://whc.unesco.org/en/list/1100.
73. Channel, H. *Famous Stari Most Bridge Collapses In Bosnia*. 1993 [cited 2020 14/05]; Available from: https://www.historychannel.com.au/this-day-in-history/famous-stari-most-bridge-collapses-in-bosnia/.

74. Ultimate Kilimanjaro. *Which Route Should I Use to Climb Kilimanjaro?* 2019 [cited 2020 14/05]; Available from: https://www.ultimatekilimanjaro.com/routes.htm.
75. Conover, E., *Climbing Mount Kilimanjaro*. 2018.
76. Singh, U.M., B. Gurubacharya, and E. Schmall. *Overcrowding on Mount Everest contributes to rise in deaths*. 2019 [cited 2020 14/05]; Available from: https://www.pbs.org/newshour/world/overcrowding-on-mount-everest-contributes-to-rise-in-deaths.
77. App Spring, I. *150 Most Famous Landmarks in the World*. 2019 [cited 2020 13/04]; Available from: https://www.listchallenges.com/150-most-famous-landmarks-in-the-world.
78. UNESCO. *Tasmanian Wilderness*. 1982 [cited 2020 17/05]; Available from: https://whc.unesco.org/en/list/181.
79. UNESCO. *Mount Taishan*. 2015 [cited 2020 31/05]; Available from: https://whc.unesco.org/en/list/437/.
80. Goldberger, P., *Why Architecture Matters*. 2009: Yale University Press.
81. Jencks, C.A., *The Language of Post-Modern Architecture.* Journal of Aesthetics and Art Criticism, 1978. **37**(2): p. 239-240.
82. Summerson, J., *The classical language of architecture / John Summerson*. 1964, London: Methuen.
83. Appleyard, D., *Why buildings are known : a predictive tool for architects and planners*.

1969, Berkeley: Institute of Urban & Regional Development, University of California.
84. Harriss, J., *The tallest tower : Eiffel and the Belle Epoque*. 1975, Boston: Boston : Houghton Mifflin.
85. Smithfield, B. *Guy de Maupassant ate lunch everyday at the base of The Eiffel Tower*. 2016 [cited 2020 26/04]; Available from: https://www.thevintagenews.com/2016/09/20/priority-french-writer-ate-lunch-everyday-base-eiffel-tower-place-paris-not-see-2/.
86. Brown, S.L. *Hidden Vault: Tributes to 'Yellow Peril' sculpture dound in public places across Melbourne*. 2016 [cited 2020 26/04]; Available from: https://www.abc.net.au/news/2016-04-05/vault-yellow-peril-sculpture-tributes-scattered-across-melbourne/7248702.
87. Wallis, G.J., *Peril in the Square: The Sculpture that Challenged a City*, in *The Age*. 2004.
88. Glancey, J. *Soaring above Barcelona, Antonio Gaudí's church will eventually become the world's tallest when it is finally finished*. 2014 [cited 2020 30/05]; Available from: https://www.bbc.com/culture/article/20141014-gaudi-unfinished-business.
89. West-Knights, I., *Was the Millennium Dome really so bad? The inside story of a (not so) total disaster*, in *The Guardian*. 2020.
90. Ward. *On this day in history in 1894, Blackpool Tower was opened*. 2006 [cited 2020 12/05]; Available from: https://www.wardsbookofdays.com/14may.htm.
91. McGrath, K. *50 Iconic Buildings Around the World You Need to See Before You Die*. 2017

[cited 2020 18/05]; Available from: https://www.architecturaldigest.com/story/most-iconic-buildings-around-the-world.

92. Hello Magazine. *Top 12 must-see landmarks in the world for 2019*. 2019 [cited 2019 13/04]; Available from: https://www.hellomagazine.com/travel/2019020167299/top-world-landmarks/.

93. As stated. *Basilica of the Sagrada Familia*. 2019 [cited 2020 15/05]; Available from: https://www.tripadvisor.com.au/Attraction_Review-g187497-d190166-Reviews-Basilica_of_the_Sagrada_Familia-Barcelona_Catalonia.html.

94. Oberhelman, D., *Stanford Encyclopedia of Philosophy*. Reference Reviews, 2001. **15**(6): p. 9-9.

95. Editors, H.C. *Hagia Sophia*. 2018 [cited 2020 8/06]; Available from: https://www.history.com/topics/ancient-greece/hagia-sophia.

96. National Museum Australia. *Sydney Harbour Bridge opens*. 2020 [cited 2020 23/06]; Available from: https://www.nma.gov.au/defining-moments/resources/sydney-harbour-bridge-opens.

97. Graham, B. *New digital images show what Sydney Harbour Bridge outtakes would have looked like*. 2019 [cited 2020 9/06]; Available from: https://www.news.com.au/technology/innovation/design/new-digital-images-show-what-sydney-harbour-bridge-outtakes-would-have-

looked-like/news-story/94973b600a5edf8835821c2be67ad289.

98. Hunter, W. *The Story Behind the Poem on the Statue of Liberty*. 2018 [cited 2020 12/06]; Available from: https://www.theatlantic.com/entertainment/archive/2018/01/the-story-behind-the-poem-on-the-statue-of-liberty/550553/.

About the Author

Christopher J. Elliott is an urban designer working in the field of tourism for over thirty years. He has a Master of Arts in Tourism, a Master of Urban Design and a Bachelor of Landscape Architecture. He has developed attractions in over twenty countries and learnt from successes and failures across Asia, North America, the Middle East, Europe and Australia.

Author Contact

Email: christopher.je@gmail.com

Linkedin: https://www.linkedin.com/in/christopher-elliott-b554942a/

Acknowledgments

Many thanks to Lauren Mullings, Geoff Williams and Christopher Tan for your support and help with this book. Thank you to Monash University Tourism Department, Victoria Peel, Jeff Jarvis, Madelene Blaer and Joseph Cheer, as well the tutors and my tram friends for persevering with my many questions. Thank you to Julie Postance and editor Amanda J Spedding. Inspiration for this book came from my many friends at HOK, Tract, Spiire and the City of Melbourne as well as the previously named companies of EDAW and Planisphere. Thank you to Kate Dundas, Bronagh Kennedy, Bill Hanway, Jason Prior, Steve Townsend, Scott Dunn and Sylvester Wong for enabling the many urban design stories I have experienced around the world. Most of all thankyou to Akit Fong who drove me forward through better and worse moments.

www.ingramcontent.com/pod-product-compliance
Lightning Source LLC
Chambersburg PA
CBHW010245010526
44107CB00063B/2682